CHER

NEW M...

2024

The Untold Story of Music, Fame, Reinvention, and an Icon's Unstoppable Journey

---

CLAIRE MORSE

Copyright Notice

© 2024 **CLAIRE MORSE**. All rights reserved.

No part of this publication may be reproduced, distributed, or transmitted in any form or by any means, including photocopying, recording, or other electronic or mechanical methods, without the prior written permission of the publisher, except in the case of brief quotations embodied in reviews or certain other non-commercial uses permitted by copyright law. For permission requests, write to the publisher at the address below:

Disclaimer

This book is a work of non-fiction, based on publicly available information, personal interviews, and shared accounts from individuals closely associated with Kim Porter. While every effort has been made to ensure accuracy, certain details have been reconstructed based on memory and interpretation. Names, events, and places mentioned in this book are true to the best of the author's knowledge, but some conversations, thoughts, and personal perspectives may have been altered or combined for narrative coherence.

CONTENTS

Foreword 6

Introduction 8

1 13

    The Early Days.. 13

        Humble Beginnings in El Centro, California 13

        Growing Up with Big Dreams 16

        Growing Up with Big Dreams 19

        The First Glimpse of Stardom 23

2 27

    Meeting Sonny Bono 27

        A Chance Encounter that Changed Everything 27

        The Birth of Sonny & Cher 34

        "I Got You Babe" and the World's Spotlight 39

3 44

    The Sonny & Cher Era 44

        Taking Over the Charts 44

        The Sonny & Cher Comedy Hour 49

Behind the Glamour 54

4 60

Breaking Out as a Solo Artist 60

Finding Her Own Voice 60

Early Hits and Misses 65

Reinventing Herself in the 1970s 69

5 75

The Hollywood Years 75

A Natural Actress Emerges 75

Breakout Roles in Silkwood and Mask 80

Winning an Oscar for Moonstruck 82

6 86

Reinvention in the 1980s and 1990s 86

The Queen of Comebacks 86

Fashion, Fame, and Fearlessness 90

The Birth of "Believe" and a New Era of Music 93

7 98

A Voice for Change 98

Advocating for LGBTQ+ Rights 98

Humanitarian Work and Philanthropy 102

Speaking Out in a Changing World 106

8 111

Cher the Icon 111

Her Influence on Fashion and Style 111

Staying Relevant Through Decades 116

Inspiring a New Generation 121

9 126

Love and Family 126

Marriages and Relationships 126

Raising Children in the Spotlight 130

The Bond with Her Late Mother, Georgia Holt 135

10 140

Cher Today 140

Life Beyond the Spotlight 140

New Projects and Ventures 144

Cher's Legacy 149

Conclusion 154

Foreword

When we think of a true icon, one name that inevitably comes to mind is Cher. Few individuals have so seamlessly transcended generations, reinventing themselves while remaining an unwavering force of nature. Her story is not just one of talent but of resilience, transformation, and an unyielding belief in one's own voice. As we gather to explore her extraordinary life, we find ourselves drawn into a narrative that is as inspiring as it is unparalleled.

This book is more than a recounting of Cher's accomplishments; it is a tribute to her spirit. Together, we will journey through the highs and lows, the triumphs and tribulations, and the countless reinventions that have made Cher the powerhouse she is today. From a small-town girl with big dreams to a global sensation who has forever left her mark on music, film, and fashion, Cher's story is one that reminds us all of the boundless possibilities life can hold when we dare to be fearless.

As you turn these pages, let yourself be inspired by the grit, glamour, and glory of Cher. May her journey encourage each of us to embrace our own potential, to stand tall in the face of adversity, and to believe, as she does, that the best is always yet to come. Her legacy is not only a testament to her greatness but an invitation for all of us to dream bigger and shine brighter.

So let us begin this celebration of a life lived boldly and authentically. Cher's story is not just hers alone; it belongs to all of us who dare to believe in the power of reinvention and the magic of staying true to oneself.

Introduction

"Until you're ready to look foolish, you'll never have the possibility of being great." These words, famously spoken by Cher, encapsulate the daring spirit that has defined her life and career. Born Cherilyn Sarkisian in 1946, Cher emerged from modest beginnings to become one of the most enduring and versatile figures in entertainment. Her story is not just a chronicle of talent and ambition but a testament to perseverance, reinvention, and fearless authenticity that has left an indelible mark on music, film, and pop culture.

Cher's impact is monumental, spanning decades in an industry notorious for its fleeting attention. She isn't merely a performer; she's a phenomenon. From her first appearance as half of the iconic duo Sonny & Cher to her groundbreaking solo career, her contributions have transcended the confines of entertainment. Cher has proven time and again that she is more than a voice, a face, or a style—she is a symbol of transformation, strength, and individuality.

In the 1960s, Cher and Sonny Bono's infectious hit "I Got You Babe" catapulted them into the limelight, defining an era with their unique sound and bohemian image. Yet Cher's journey was only beginning. As the duo's career flourished, so did her star power, making her not just a singer but a household name. The Sonny & Cher Comedy Hour showcased her wit and charisma, demonstrating that she was more than a singer—she was a natural entertainer.

When the Sonny & Cher era came to an end, many assumed Cher's career would fade with it. Instead, she defied expectations. The 1970s marked her first major reinvention, where she boldly stepped out as a solo artist. Her albums during this period were a mix of hits and experimentation, but Cher's grit and determination never wavered. She was learning, evolving, and building the foundation for her next breakthrough.

By the 1980s, Cher was ready to conquer a new frontier: Hollywood. Her acting career began modestly, but her persistence paid off. Critics and audiences alike took notice of her dramatic chops in *Silkwood* (1983), where she held her own alongside acting heavyweights like Meryl Streep. Her performance earned her an Academy Award nomination and marked the beginning of a new chapter. This newfound respect as a serious actress culminated in her Oscar-winning role in *Moonstruck* (1987). In a performance as Loretta Castorini, Cher captivated the world with her charm and emotional depth, proving once and for all that she was a master of reinvention.

Cher's ability to shift gears and thrive in new arenas is one of the most compelling aspects of her story. While many artists peak in one medium, she continued to diversify. Even as her acting career soared, Cher remained a force in music. The late 1980s saw her return to the charts with powerful rock anthems like "If I Could Turn Back Time." This era marked yet another evolution in her sound and image, as she embraced bold styles and daring performances that kept audiences mesmerized.

Perhaps one of Cher's most remarkable achievements came in the late 1990s when she revolutionized the music industry with her dance-pop anthem "Believe." Released in 1998, the song not only topped charts worldwide but also introduced autotune as a stylistic tool, forever changing the landscape of pop music. At a time when many of her contemporaries had long since faded from public consciousness, Cher was once again at the forefront, setting trends and dominating airwaves.

Cher's influence extends far beyond her music and acting. She has become a fashion icon, known for her audacious red-carpet looks and collaborations with designer Bob Mackie. Her style choices have been as fearless as her career moves, challenging norms and redefining glamour on her terms. Whether she was dazzling audiences in her iconic feathered headdresses or sparking conversation with bold, barely-there ensembles, Cher's fashion has always been a statement of empowerment and individuality.

Beyond her professional achievements, Cher's personal journey has also resonated deeply with fans. Her openness about her struggles and triumphs has made her relatable and inspiring. From navigating her parents' divorce in childhood to weathering her own high-profile relationships and challenges, Cher has shown that vulnerability and strength are not mutually exclusive. Her candor about the ups and downs of her life has made her a beacon of resilience for those facing their own battles.

In addition to her artistic and personal milestones, Cher has also made significant contributions as an activist and philanthropist. Over the years, she has used her platform to advocate for causes close to her heart, from LGBTQ+ rights to veterans' welfare. Her work in these areas reflects her belief in using her voice to make a difference, cementing her legacy as not just an entertainer but also a humanitarian.

Cher's ability to stay relevant across generations is nothing short of extraordinary. In an industry that often favors the young and new, she has defied the odds by remaining a cultural touchstone for more than six decades. Whether through her electrifying Las Vegas residencies, her ventures into Broadway, or her continued presence in film and music, Cher has consistently proven that age is no barrier to innovation or excellence.

The story of Cher is a celebration of individuality and the courage to embrace change. She has shown the world that reinvention is not a sign of inconsistency but a testament to growth and adaptability. By refusing to be boxed into one identity or defined by one moment, Cher has crafted a career that is as dynamic and multifaceted as the woman herself.

As you explore further into her life through the chapters of this book, you will discover not just an entertainer but a trailblazer who dared to defy conventions. You will see a woman who has broken barriers, inspired millions, and carved out a legacy that will endure for generations to come. Cher's story is one of unwavering determination, boundless creativity, and a relentless pursuit of excellence—a story that continues to captivate and inspire.

1

The Early Days

Humble Beginnings in El Centro, California

Born on May 20, 1946, in El Centro, California, Cherilyn Sarkisian came into the world with no immediate indication that she would one day become one of the most iconic figures in the history of entertainment. El Centro, a small town in Southern California, was far removed from the glamour of Hollywood or the bright lights of the music industry. Cher's early life was far from the luxury and fame that would later define her; instead, it was marked by challenges, instability, and a deep desire to escape the ordinary.

Cher's parents, John and Georgia, were both ambitious individuals, but their relationship was tumultuous. Her father, a truck driver, was often absent from the household, leaving Georgia to raise Cher and her half-sister, Georganne, mostly on her own. Georgia was a talented singer, and although she dreamed of making it big, she struggled to find her footing in the entertainment industry. Despite this, Cher's mother instilled in her a love for music from an early age. Georgia would sing around the house, and it was from her that Cher first experienced the power of music as an emotional escape and a path to self-expression.

From a very young age, Cher was aware that her family's situation was far from ideal. Her parents' marriage was unstable, and they would eventually separate when she was just ten years old. This disruption in her home life had a profound impact on Cher. She later described her childhood as one filled with confusion and uncertainty. Moving from place to place, sometimes living with relatives and sometimes in a series of cramped apartments, Cher often found solace in music, using it as a way to cope with the emotional turbulence surrounding her.

One of Cher's earliest memories is of her mother singing along to the radio while they worked around the house. Even as a young girl, Cher was captivated by music and the idea of performing. However, her confidence was not always as strong as her dreams. Cher struggled with self-doubt and often found herself feeling like an outsider. As she grew older, her natural beauty began to blossom, and she would frequently get attention for her striking looks, but she also began to sense that there was something special about her—something that would push her beyond the confines of her small town.

Cher's path to stardom was anything but straightforward. Despite her longing for fame, her early life was not glamorous. As a teenager, she was very much the product of her circumstances. She wasn't handed opportunities, and she certainly didn't have a clear path to success. But what she did have was an unshakeable determination to rise above her surroundings. She dropped out of high school at the age of 16 and moved to Los Angeles in pursuit of a career in entertainment, knowing full well that the journey would be long and challenging.

It was in Los Angeles that Cher truly began to understand the business of show business. She spent time working odd jobs to support herself, all the while taking every opportunity to learn the ins and outs of the entertainment industry. It was during this time that she crossed paths with a man who would change her life forever: Sonny Bono. But before their famous partnership, Cher spent time in the city auditioning for various roles and trying to find her way.

In a way, Cher's early life in El Centro and the struggles she faced as a young adult would become the foundation for everything she would later achieve. She learned early on that success wasn't handed to you—it was earned, often through persistence and a refusal to accept defeat. This mindset would define her entire career, helping her navigate the often difficult and unpredictable world of entertainment.

The early days of Cher's life were not easy, and yet they were crucial to the person she would become. She had a drive and ambition that were fueled by her desire to escape the limitations of her upbringing. But more than that, Cher learned the importance of reinvention and resilience—lessons that would serve her well in the years to come. Even in the most difficult moments, Cher held onto her dream of becoming something more, a dream that, in time, would become a reality.

Growing Up with Big Dreams

Growing up, Cherilyn Sarkisian always felt like she was destined for something bigger than the small-town life she knew in El Centro, California. Even as a young girl, Cher stood out. Her exotic looks—dark hair, almond-shaped eyes, and a striking bone structure—set her apart from her peers, but it wasn't just her appearance that made her different. Cher had a restless energy, an unshakable sense that she was meant for more, even if she didn't yet know what "more" looked like.

Cher's early years were marked by a blend of struggle and aspiration. Her mother, Georgia Holt, was a significant influence in her life. Georgia, a talented singer and occasional actress, instilled in Cher a love for music and the arts. Although Georgia's own dreams of stardom never fully materialized, she encouraged her daughter to dream big, teaching her that it was okay to reach for something beyond the ordinary. However, life in the Sarkisian household wasn't without its difficulties. Financial instability meant frequent moves and constant adjustments to new schools and neighborhoods, which left Cher feeling like an outsider.

As a child, Cher grappled with feelings of insecurity. She struggled academically due to undiagnosed dyslexia, which made school a daunting experience. This learning difficulty, coupled with her family's frequent relocations, left her feeling isolated. Despite these challenges, Cher found solace in performing. She would entertain herself—and anyone who would watch—with dramatic reenactments and impromptu singing sessions. From a young age, she displayed a flair for the theatrical, often imagining herself as the star of her own show.

Television and movies became a window into a world far removed from her own reality. Cher was mesmerized by the glamour and allure of Hollywood. She idolized stars like Audrey Hepburn and Marilyn Monroe, dreaming of one day becoming a part of that world. She would spend hours in front of the mirror, imitating their mannerisms, practicing their lines, and imagining herself walking the red carpet. Even then, she was laying the foundation for the bold, unapologetic persona that would later captivate millions.

Cher's ambitions were fueled by a sense of urgency. She wasn't content to wait for life to happen to her; she wanted to take control of her destiny. Her restlessness became more pronounced in her teenage years, when she began to feel constrained by the limitations of her small-town life. She often talked about leaving El Centro and moving to Los Angeles, where she believed opportunities awaited. Her friends and family sometimes dismissed these dreams as fanciful, but Cher never wavered in her belief that she was destined for something extraordinary.

During her adolescence, Cher's unique sense of style began to emerge. While other girls wore traditional outfits, Cher experimented with bold fashion choices, often repurposing old clothes to create something entirely her own. Her unconventional style was a reflection of her personality—fearless, creative, and unwilling to conform to societal norms. These early experiments with fashion would later become a hallmark of her career, as she continually pushed boundaries and set trends.

Despite her big dreams, Cher's path was not without obstacles. Her parents' divorce meant that she often had to step up and take on responsibilities at home. These experiences forced her to grow up quickly, but they also instilled in her a sense of resilience. She learned to adapt, to find her way in uncertain circumstances, and to hold onto her dreams no matter what challenges came her way.

By the time Cher was a teenager, she had set her sights firmly on a future in entertainment. She knew that staying in El Centro would mean a life of mediocrity, and that was something she simply couldn't accept. At the age of 16, she made the bold decision to drop out of high school and move to Los Angeles. It was a leap of faith, driven by her belief in herself and her determination to carve out a place in the world.

Cher's childhood and adolescence were a testament to the power of dreaming big, even in the face of adversity. She wasn't born into privilege or opportunity, but she possessed an unrelenting drive to change her circumstances. Growing up, she may not have had a clear blueprint for success, but she had something even more valuable: a belief in her own potential. That belief, coupled with her extraordinary talent and determination, would soon propel her into a world she had only imagined.

Growing Up with Big Dreams

Growing up with big dreams meant that Cherilyn Sarkisian, a young girl from El Centro, California, always looked beyond her immediate surroundings. Cher's life as a child was not one of luxury or ease. Her family struggled financially, moving from place to place in search of stability. Despite these challenges, Cher's imagination soared. Her dreams were as expansive as the sky above the California desert where she grew up, and she never doubted that her future held something extraordinary.

Raised primarily by her mother, Georgia Holt, Cher learned early on the value of perseverance and determination. Georgia, a talented singer and actress, worked tirelessly to provide for her family while nurturing her own ambitions. Though Georgia faced countless setbacks, she never let go of her dreams—and she passed that indomitable spirit on to her daughter. For young Cher, her mother's resilience was both an inspiration and a lesson: success didn't come easily, but it was worth fighting for.

Cher's early years were filled with moments that hinted at her future in entertainment. She was drawn to music, often singing along to records her mother played at home. Her voice, even as a child, carried a unique timbre—deep, rich, and emotional. But music wasn't her only passion. She was captivated by the glamour of Hollywood, spending hours watching classic films and imagining herself on the silver screen. She idolized stars like Audrey Hepburn and Marilyn Monroe, often mimicking their elegance and charisma in front of the mirror.

In school, Cher struggled academically, partly due to undiagnosed dyslexia. Reading and writing were difficult for her, and this led to feelings of inadequacy and frustration. But where traditional education seemed to fail her, her creative instincts flourished. Cher excelled in storytelling, dramatizing everyday situations, and captivating anyone who would listen. Her charisma and natural ability to command attention became evident, even as a child. She didn't just dream of performing—she lived it in her daily life.

Cher's self-expression extended to her sense of style, which began to develop during her adolescence. While other girls adhered to the latest trends, Cher experimented with bold, unconventional looks. She enjoyed standing out, whether through dramatic makeup, unique hairstyles, or hand-altered clothes. This fearless approach to fashion reflected her larger-than-life dreams and her refusal to conform. Even then, she was unknowingly laying the groundwork for her future as a fashion icon.

The limitations of her small-town environment only fueled her ambitions. While many of her peers were content with the familiarity of El Centro, Cher longed for the excitement of the big city. She would often tell anyone who would listen about her plans to leave and make a name for herself in Los Angeles. Her friends admired her determination, though some doubted whether such big dreams were realistic. But Cher was undeterred. She didn't just want to escape her circumstances—she wanted to transform her life entirely.

As she entered her teenage years, Cher's sense of purpose became even stronger. She began to see herself not just as a dreamer, but as someone capable of making those dreams a reality. Her decision to drop out of high school at 16 was not made lightly. It was a bold move, born out of her conviction that the traditional path wasn't meant for her. Cher didn't see her dyslexia or her struggles in school as failures; instead, she viewed them as signs that her talents lay elsewhere. She trusted her instincts, and her instincts told her that her future awaited in Los Angeles.

Cher's big dreams weren't just fantasies—they were plans. She envisioned herself singing on grand stages, starring in blockbuster films, and living a life of creativity and expression. What set her apart was her willingness to act on those dreams, even when the odds seemed stacked against her. She wasn't afraid of taking risks or stepping into the unknown, because she believed in her ability to make things happen.

Looking back, Cher's childhood and adolescence were defined by a sense of destiny. She was a girl with big dreams, but more importantly, she was a girl who refused to let go of them. Every challenge she faced, from financial struggles to academic difficulties, became fuel for her ambition. She didn't just dream of a better life—she made it her mission to create one.

The First Glimpse of Stardom

The first glimpse of stardom came to Cher in a way that seemed almost fated, as though the universe conspired to align her with the path she was meant to walk. It was 1962 when a wide-eyed 16-year-old Cherilyn Sarkisian left El Centro for Los Angeles. With little more than her dreams, a vibrant personality, and an innate belief in her potential, she was determined to turn her fantasies into reality.

Los Angeles, with its bustling streets and endless possibilities, was both thrilling and intimidating. The city was a far cry from her quiet upbringing, but Cher embraced it wholeheartedly. She found herself drawn to the glamour and grit of Hollywood, often wandering the streets, soaking in the energy of a city that promised fame and fortune to those brave enough to chase it.

Her journey into stardom began with a chance meeting that would change her life forever. While living with a friend and scraping by, Cher met Sonny Bono, a charismatic and ambitious man who was already navigating the music industry. Their connection was immediate and undeniable. Sonny, who worked for music producer Phil Spector, saw something in Cher that others hadn't yet recognized. It wasn't just her striking appearance or her deep, soulful voice—it was her raw potential, her hunger for success, and her ability to command attention effortlessly.

Sonny became both a mentor and a partner, helping Cher secure her first work as a backup singer for Spector's legendary productions. These were the early 1960s, a golden era for pop music, and Cher's voice could be heard on hits like "Be My Baby" by The Ronettes and "You've Lost That Lovin' Feelin'" by The Righteous Brothers. Though her contributions were behind the scenes, they marked her first steps into the music industry. She was learning, growing, and finding her place in a competitive world.

Sonny and Cher's relationship quickly evolved into a personal and professional partnership. Sonny believed in Cher's talent and encouraged her to step out from the shadows of backup singing to pursue a solo career. Cher was hesitant at first, doubting her ability to carry a song on her own. But Sonny's unwavering confidence in her proved to be a turning point. With his support, Cher began recording her first solo tracks, experimenting with her vocal style and developing the confidence that would later define her performances.

In 1965, the duo released their first hit single, *"I Got You Babe."* The song, written by Sonny, was a love anthem that resonated with a generation. Cher's rich contralto voice paired perfectly with Sonny's tenor, creating a unique sound that was both timeless and fresh. The song's success was meteoric, catapulting Sonny and Cher into the spotlight. They became instant stars, known for their chemistry, their distinctive style, and their undeniable charm.

For Cher, this was the first real taste of fame. She relished the attention and the opportunities that came with it, but she also understood that success was fleeting if not carefully nurtured. She worked tirelessly, perfecting her craft and adapting to the demands of stardom. Performing live was both exhilarating and terrifying, but Cher thrived under the pressure. Each performance was a chance to connect with her audience, to share a piece of herself, and to solidify her place in the industry.

Cher's fashion choices during this period also became a defining aspect of her early stardom. She embraced bold, unconventional outfits that challenged traditional norms, setting her apart from other artists of the era. Her unique sense of style—often featuring fringe, sequins, and daring cuts—captivated fans and critics alike, establishing her as a fashion trendsetter. Even in the earliest stages of her career, Cher demonstrated her ability to innovate and stand out, traits that would define her legacy.

As their fame grew, Sonny and Cher became household names. They released a string of hits, including *"The Beat Goes On"* and *"Baby Don't Go,"* and starred in their own television variety show, *The Sonny & Cher Comedy Hour.* Cher's sharp wit and infectious personality shone through, endearing her to millions of viewers.

Though Sonny often took the lead in their public appearances, it was clear that Cher was the real star in the making.

This period marked the beginning of Cher's journey into stardom—a time when her dreams of fame were no longer just dreams but a burgeoning reality. It was a time of firsts: her first hit song, her first television appearances, and her first experiences with the pressures and privileges of fame.

Looking back, it's clear that these early years were crucial in shaping Cher into the icon she would become. They were years of discovery, growth, and determination, proving that her dreams were not only valid but achievable. Cher was no longer just a girl with big dreams; she was a star on the rise, ready to conquer the world.

2

Meeting Sonny Bono

A Chance Encounter that Changed Everything

S ome people meet their destiny by chance; others create it step by step. For Cher, destiny walked through the door in the form of Sonny Bono."

In 1962, Cherilyn Sarkisian was just another teenage girl in Los Angeles, chasing dreams of stardom with wide eyes and boundless energy. The city, with its sprawling streets and glittering promises, had attracted countless hopefuls, and she was no exception. At just 16, she already stood out with her striking looks, husky voice, and a charisma that seemed impossible to overlook. Little did she know, her journey toward fame and fortune was about to intersect with someone who would forever change her life.

Cher met Sonny Bono in the most unassuming of circumstances. Sonny was working for Phil Spector, the legendary music producer behind some of the era's biggest hits. Sonny wasn't a famous singer or performer, but he had a reputation for being resourceful, driven, and deeply connected to the burgeoning music scene. At the time, he was juggling jobs, working behind the scenes to make ends meet while building his own dreams in the industry.

When Cher and Sonny first crossed paths, it wasn't love at first sight in the traditional sense. Sonny was 27, a full 11 years older than Cher, and already married. Cher, by contrast, was a headstrong teenager who had little interest in convention or societal expectations. Yet, their chemistry was undeniable. It wasn't romantic at first; instead, it was the kind of magnetic pull that two like-minded dreamers feel when they meet.

Sonny saw something in Cher that others had overlooked. To him, she wasn't just another pretty girl hoping to make it big—she was a rare talent with a voice that could cut through the noise of any room. But it wasn't just her voice that captivated Sonny; it was her presence. Cher had an innate ability to command attention without trying, a natural confidence that suggested she was destined for greatness.

Cher, on the other hand, found in Sonny a mentor, a guide, and a partner. Where she was raw and unpolished, Sonny was experienced and pragmatic. He understood the ins and outs of the music business, and he was eager to share that knowledge with someone he believed could go far. Their relationship, though unconventional, became a powerful partnership.

Cher later admitted that she was drawn to Sonny not just for his connections but for his unwavering belief in her abilities. It was Sonny who encouraged her to pursue music seriously, convincing her that she had the talent and drive to make it. He wasn't just supportive; he was relentless in pushing her to step out of her comfort zone. When Cher doubted herself—a common occurrence in those early days—Sonny was there to reassure her, to remind her that she had something unique to offer.

Their collaboration began modestly. Sonny invited Cher to work as a backup singer on tracks produced by Phil Spector. These sessions marked her first real exposure to the professional music scene, and though she wasn't the star, she was learning quickly. Working with Spector was no small feat; he was a perfectionist known for his "Wall of Sound" production style, and every session was an intense, high-stakes experience. Cher, however, thrived in this environment. Her voice added depth and character to the recordings, earning her recognition among her peers.

It was during these early sessions that Sonny and Cher's bond deepened. They weren't just colleagues; they were becoming inseparable. Sonny took Cher under his wing, helping her navigate the complexities of the music industry while also serving as her biggest cheerleader. Cher, in turn, brought out a softer, more creative side in Sonny. Together, they were a team, and their shared ambitions began to take shape.

As their professional relationship grew, so did their personal connection. Sonny's marriage eventually ended, and his relationship with Cher blossomed into something more romantic. Though the age difference raised eyebrows, neither of them paid much attention to the critics. They were too focused on building their future together to care about what others thought.

Sonny and Cher's dynamic was unique. Sonny was the visionary, the strategist who laid out the path they would follow. Cher, meanwhile, was the star, the one who would light up the stage and captivate audiences. But their roles weren't rigid. Sonny often performed alongside Cher, showcasing a chemistry that was both endearing and electric. They complemented each other perfectly, each bringing strengths that elevated the other.

Their first major breakthrough as a duo came with the release of *"Baby Don't Go"* in 1964. The song, written by Sonny, was a modest hit that showcased Cher's rich, emotive voice. It wasn't a blockbuster success, but it was enough to get them noticed. For Cher, it was the first taste of what was possible, a glimpse of the stardom she had always dreamed of.

By this point, Sonny and Cher were no longer just partners—they were a brand. They adopted a bohemian look that set them apart from the polished, cookie-cutter acts of the time. Sonny, with his shaggy hair and eccentric outfits, and Cher, with her striking features and bold fashion choices, became instant icons. They weren't just musicians; they were trendsetters, embodying a countercultural spirit that resonated with the youth of the 1960s.

The real turning point came in 1965 with the release of *"I Got You Babe."* The song was a phenomenon, a chart-topping hit that defined a generation. The infectious melody, combined with Cher's deep, soulful voice and Sonny's warm tenor, struck a chord with listeners across the world. "I Got You Babe" wasn't just a song—it was a declaration. It was the anthem of a couple united by love, and it reflected the spirit of the times. The song's success elevated Sonny and Cher from up-and-coming artists to international superstars.

For Cher, it was a transformative moment. The song's success brought them unprecedented attention and cemented her place in the public consciousness. What began as a shared dream with Sonny was now a reality. She wasn't just another backup singer or struggling artist—she was a part of one of the most beloved musical duos of the 1960s. Their performances were electric, drawing large crowds, and their chemistry on stage was undeniable. The public couldn't get enough of them.

But it wasn't just the music that captivated audiences. Sonny and Cher's personal relationship played a significant role in their rise to fame. Their dynamic was both charming and relatable, especially to young couples who admired the authenticity of their connection. Cher, with her undeniable presence and unique fashion sense, quickly became a style icon, while Sonny played the role of the supportive partner, always encouraging Cher's success.

The public loved their realness, their authenticity, and their refusal to conform to the norms of the entertainment industry. Together, they represented something more than just a musical act—they represented a cultural shift. They were a symbol of the growing counterculture movement, a time when norms were being challenged, and individuality was being celebrated.

Their newfound fame also opened doors to new opportunities. In 1966, they became the stars of their own TV show, *The Sonny & Cher Comedy Hour*. The show was a mixture of comedy sketches, music performances, and lighthearted banter, and it was a major hit. Cher, who had grown up watching television and dreaming of being on screen, now found herself not only singing but also acting and entertaining in a whole new way.

Cher's comedic timing, paired with her striking beauty and the couple's playful chemistry, made the show an instant success. The show's success also introduced her to a wider audience, showcasing her versatility as an entertainer. She was no longer just a pop star—she was a full-fledged television personality, adored by millions.

The show's popularity only added to the pressure on their personal relationship. As their professional lives flourished, their marriage began to fray. The long hours of working together, combined with the strains of their rising fame, began to take a toll. Despite their undeniable bond and shared goals, the demands of their careers and their differing personalities started to create tension. Cher's growing independence and Sonny's need for control were factors that contributed to their eventual separation.

But even as their personal relationship began to unravel, their professional partnership continued to thrive. They had already built a legacy together, and their influence in both music and television would remain for years to come. Cher had always been the star, but it was Sonny who had been the architect of their success, pushing her to take risks and grow as an artist.

Looking back, it's clear that their meeting was more than just a chance encounter—it was a convergence of two individuals who were destined to change the face of entertainment. Sonny's belief in Cher's talent and his unwavering commitment to helping her achieve her dreams played a critical role in her rise to stardom. But Cher's innate star power, her determination, and her ability to captivate audiences ensured that their partnership would leave a lasting impact.

For Cher, meeting Sonny Bono was the beginning of everything. It was the moment that set her on the path to superstardom. But it was also the start of a partnership that would shape her for the rest of her life, both professionally and personally. Their time together, though filled with highs and lows, created a foundation that Cher would continue to build upon for decades. It was a moment of fate that not only launched her career but also set her on a journey toward becoming one of the most iconic figures in the entertainment world.

The Birth of Sonny & Cher

The birth of Sonny and Cher as a musical and cultural phenomenon was not just a merger of talent but a blend of personalities, ambition, and vision that resonated deeply with audiences of the 1960s. When Sonny Bono and Cherilyn Sarkisian joined forces, it was a union of more than just two people; it was the creation of an iconic duo that would redefine the pop music landscape and become symbols of a generation.

At the heart of their partnership was the recognition that they complemented each other perfectly. Sonny, with his shrewd understanding of the music industry, saw in Cher a raw talent that could not be ignored. Though she had yet to develop the polished persona that would eventually define her, Cher possessed an unmistakable voice and presence that Sonny believed could captivate the world. On the other hand, Cher, with her tenacity and instinctive star quality, trusted Sonny to help guide her through the complexities of the music business, even if their dynamic was not always without friction.

The duo's first real hit came in 1965 with the release of "I Got You Babe." The song's success was both immediate and overwhelming, climbing to number one on the Billboard charts and marking the start of a career that would evolve beyond music. What made "I Got You Babe" so special wasn't just its catchy melody or the harmonizing voices of Sonny and Cher—it was the emotional honesty that both artists brought to the track. Cher's deep, soulful contralto voice blended effortlessly with Sonny's lighter tenor, creating a contrast that felt both fresh and timeless.

The success of "I Got You Babe" catapulted the pair into the spotlight, making them household names virtually overnight.

They weren't just another pop duo; they were a cultural force. Their image was new, exciting, and rebellious in a way that resonated with the changing social and political landscape of the 1960s. Their long, flowing hair, bohemian fashion choices, and unapologetic authenticity spoke to the growing counterculture movement that was taking hold among young people at the time.

Their performances were a spectacle in their own right. Cher, who had previously been a backup singer, now stood front and center, basking in the adoration of thousands of fans. Sonny, with his distinct style and larger-than-life personality, played the role of the earnest, supportive partner. The two of them were magnetic together, and their on-stage chemistry was undeniable. It wasn't just the music that captivated audiences—it was the sheer energy and connection they shared, which was palpable during every performance.

But the duo's success was not limited to their music alone. In 1966, Sonny and Cher were given their own television show, *The Sonny & Cher Comedy Hour*. The show was an instant hit, blending comedy sketches, musical performances, and banter between the couple. The mix of humor and music, along with the undeniable charm of both Sonny and Cher, made the show a perfect vehicle for them to connect with an even broader audience. Cher, in particular, proved herself to be an engaging and witty television personality. She wasn't just a pop star; she was a multifaceted entertainer, and *The Sonny & Cher Comedy Hour* allowed her to show off a different side of herself.

The show allowed Cher to further develop her comedic timing and display a charisma that was sometimes overshadowed by her musical success. Cher's chemistry with Sonny—who played the straight man to her sassy, witty persona—became one of the driving forces behind the show's success. Their easygoing interactions, combined with the mix of comedy and music, gave the audience an inside look into the dynamic of their relationship, drawing fans into their world. This blend of music and entertainment would go on to influence future television variety shows and solidified the duo as cultural icons.

But their rise to fame wasn't without its challenges. As their success continued to skyrocket, so did the pressures of stardom. The demands of constant touring, recording, and working on the television show began to take a toll on their personal relationship. Despite the obvious love and respect they had for one another, the dynamics of their professional lives began to create strains in their marriage. They were both ambitious, but their visions for the future were starting to differ. Sonny, ever the ambitious businessman, was focused on building their brand and expanding their empire. Cher, however, was increasingly interested in forging her own path, one that allowed her more creative freedom and space to explore new horizons.

Despite these growing differences, the success of Sonny and Cher's partnership continued unabated. Their music continued to top the charts, their TV show remained a fixture in households across the nation, and they became pop culture icons in every sense. Their style and music became emblematic of the era, and they were firmly entrenched in the public's consciousness as symbols of love, rebellion, and creativity. Their influence stretched far beyond the entertainment industry—Sonny and Cher became cultural icons, shaping the way people dressed, spoke, and interacted with the world around them.

Looking back, the birth of Sonny and Cher was not just about the union of two talented individuals. It was about the creation of a cultural phenomenon, a partnership that gave birth to some of the most memorable music, television, and fashion moments of the 1960s and beyond. The duo helped redefine the idea of celebrity, blending the lines between personal and professional life, and in doing so, they left an indelible mark on the world.

Their journey, full of ups and downs, was also one of discovery. For Cher, it was the realization that she had more to offer than just a beautiful voice. It was the beginning of her journey to becoming a multifaceted entertainer—one who would eventually conquer music, film, and television. For Sonny, it was the opportunity to see his vision come to life in ways he hadn't imagined. Together, they created something that was greater than the sum of its parts—a legacy that continues to influence pop culture and the entertainment industry to this day.

Sonny and Cher may have started as two individuals chasing their dreams, but together, they created something that would outlast their personal differences and grow into something much larger than themselves. Their birth as a duo wasn't just the beginning of a successful partnership—it was the start of a journey that would resonate with generations of fans and set the stage for the rest of Cher's iconic career.

'I Got You Babe' and the World's Spotlight

"I Got You Babe" wasn't just a song—it was a phenomenon. The moment it hit the airwaves in 1965, it marked a dramatic turning point in both Sonny and Cher's careers, propelling them into the stratosphere of pop stardom. The track was a perfect marriage of infectious melody, heartfelt lyrics, and the unique chemistry between the duo. What made it stand out was its raw honesty and simplicity. It was the anthem of young love—its message of support, devotion, and unity resonated with listeners, making it a timeless classic.

From the very first note, "I Got You Babe" captured the essence of the relationship between Sonny and Cher. With Sonny's light, almost whimsical voice blending with Cher's deep, soulful contralto, the song became an instant hit. Its success wasn't just a matter of chart rankings—it marked the beginning of an entirely new phase in their careers. The song hit number one on the Billboard Hot 100, staying there for several weeks, and became a signature track for the couple. It was a song that would forever define them as a duo, as it encapsulated everything about their personalities: Cher's boldness and Sonny's warmth, the union of their distinct voices, and the authenticity of their bond.

The success of "I Got You Babe" did more than just elevate their status as musicians—it thrust them into the public eye in a way they had never experienced before. Overnight, they became household names. The song played on radios across the country, in every car, every store, and every home, and it became the soundtrack to countless love stories. Cher, who had previously been a backup singer and was just beginning to carve her place in the music industry, now found herself at the center of a cultural shift. Her voice was suddenly one of the most recognized in the world, and she was no longer just a rising star—she was a pop culture icon.

Sonny, too, saw his career explode. His genius as a producer and songwriter had already earned him a respected place in the music industry, but with "I Got You Babe," he solidified his reputation as a visionary. Though he had always believed in Cher's potential, the song proved to the world that their partnership was something special. It wasn't just about the music—it was about the dynamic they created together, something that transcended their individual talents and captured the hearts of millions.

The song's success also marked the beginning of a shift in popular music. The 1960s was a time of social change, and "I Got You Babe" spoke directly to the growing counterculture movement. Its carefree, joyful tone and the theme of love and solidarity resonated deeply with the youth of the time. The hippie movement, which was gaining momentum across the United States, found an anthem in the song. It was an era of rebellion and self-expression, and "I Got You Babe" was the perfect reflection of that spirit. The song became an unofficial anthem for the youth who were rejecting the status quo and embracing individuality.

What made "I Got You Babe" even more significant was the way it captured the spirit of the time while remaining universally relatable. The simplicity of the message—that no matter what happens, love can conquer all—was a sentiment that transcended the era. It spoke to people of all ages, from the young lovers who adopted it as their theme song to the older generations who saw it as a reminder of their own romantic experiences.

For Sonny and Cher, the success of "I Got You Babe" was just the beginning. It gave them the platform they needed to build a lasting career. The song was a defining moment, but it also allowed them to explore other creative ventures. Cher, in particular, had always dreamed of expanding her horizons beyond music, and the success of the song opened doors for her to pursue acting and television. Sonny, ever the strategist, knew that they couldn't rely on just one hit. He began to strategize their next moves carefully, ensuring that their momentum was not just a passing fad but the beginning of a long, fruitful career.

The public's love for "I Got You Babe" was not just about the song—it was about what it represented. It symbolized the birth of a partnership that would go on to influence generations of artists, both in music and beyond. Sonny and Cher were no longer just two musicians—they were a symbol of something much larger. They represented the spirit of the 1960s: a time of change, of love, of rebellion, and of dreams being realized.

As their fame grew, so did the spotlight on their personal lives. The public fascination with their relationship only deepened, adding to their allure as a duo. Their every move was followed by paparazzi, and their love story became just as iconic as their music. People couldn't get enough of their dynamic, and their personal and professional lives became intertwined in ways that few celebrity couples had experienced before.

The legacy of "I Got You Babe" endures to this day. The song remains one of the most recognizable tracks of the 1960s, and it is a testament to the enduring power of love and partnership. It was a moment in time that defined an era, and it launched two of the most beloved entertainers into the world's spotlight.

For Cher, it was the beginning of her transformation from a singer to a cultural force. It marked the moment when the world first saw her potential as an artist and as an individual. Sonny, too, had found his place in the world, but it was clear that his role was not just as a musician—he was a producer, a visionary, and an integral part of the duo's success. Together, they had achieved something extraordinary, and "I Got You Babe" was their declaration to the world that they were here to stay.

In a way, "I Got You Babe" was more than just a song. It was the soundtrack to their lives, the anthem that defined not only their love story but also their rise to stardom. Through this one song, Sonny and Cher captured the hearts of millions, creating a legacy that would endure far beyond the 1960s. Their musical journey had only just begun, but "I Got You Babe" was the moment that solidified them as one of the most iconic duos in music history.

3

The Sonny & Cher Era
Taking Over the Charts

The 1960s were a time of social upheaval, cultural transformation, and musical innovation. For Sonny and Cher, it was a decade that would see them rise from relative obscurity to becoming one of the most powerful forces in the entertainment industry. With the success of "I Got You Babe," they didn't just secure a spot on the charts—they revolutionized the way music was consumed, packaged, and experienced by the public.

Their sound was unmistakable, a blend of pop, folk, and rock, with a strong dose of charm and authenticity that resonated with millions. What made Sonny and Cher stand out was their ability to transcend the typical pop duo dynamic. They weren't just performing—they were telling a story. The vulnerability in Cher's voice, combined with Sonny's earnest delivery, created a unique juxtaposition that captured the essence of the era. Their music was a reflection of the counterculture movement: raw, emotional, and unafraid to challenge the norms of mainstream society.

Following the success of "I Got You Babe," Sonny and Cher continued to dominate the charts with a string of hits that would cement their place in music history. Songs like "Baby Don't Go," "The Beat Goes On," and "Little Man" kept them at the forefront of popular music. Each track was a testament to their versatility as a duo. They weren't just one-hit wonders; they had the ability to craft songs that resonated with a wide range of audiences, from the young and rebellious to the more conservative listeners who enjoyed their catchy melodies and poignant lyrics.

The success of their singles was not just a product of their undeniable talent—it was also a result of their relentless work ethic and strategic positioning in the industry. Sonny, with his sharp business acumen, was determined to make the most of their growing fame. He understood that the music industry was about more than just talent; it was about creating a brand, and he was a master at doing just that. He pushed for the release of more singles, ensuring that they were always in the public eye. He also worked tirelessly to build their image, which was as important as their music. Sonny and Cher were no longer just a duo—they were a phenomenon, a brand that represented a particular moment in time.

As they became more famous, they also became more recognizable, not just for their music but for their fashion. The mid-to-late 1960s saw Cher's style evolve into something entirely unique. Her long, flowing hair, bohemian-inspired wardrobe, and bold fashion choices made her a trendsetter. She became a symbol of the free-spirited youth movement that was sweeping across America. Meanwhile, Sonny's look, with his dark suits, goatee, and ever-present sunglasses, became iconic in its own right. Together, they embodied the cultural shift of the 1960s, blending music with fashion, and becoming just as much a part of the visual culture as they were of the music scene.

But it wasn't just about the music or the image—it was about their chemistry. Sonny and Cher's relationship was the secret sauce that made their partnership so compelling. Their playful banter, public displays of affection, and contrasting personalities made them fascinating to watch. The way they played off each other in interviews and onstage created a sense of intimacy that drew audiences in. It was clear that they had a special bond, and people were drawn to that connection. It wasn't just their voices that harmonized—it was their relationship that made the music even more meaningful.

The couple's television career also contributed to their skyrocketing success. The launch of *The Sonny & Cher Comedy Hour* in 1971 gave them a new platform to showcase their talents, further cementing their status as a cultural phenomenon. But before that, they had already established themselves as entertainers beyond the world of music. They were everywhere—on magazine covers, in television specials, and even in movies. Their constant presence in the media created a sense of intimacy with their fans, making it feel as though they were part of their everyday lives.

As they took over the charts, their influence on the pop culture landscape was undeniable. In a time when rock 'n' roll and folk music were defining the sound of the era, Sonny and Cher managed to carve out their own niche, blending those elements into something uniquely their own. Their music became the soundtrack to a generation that was coming of age during a time of profound change. The carefree love of "I Got You Babe" resonated with a youth culture that was rejecting the rigidity of previous generations and embracing a more freewheeling, experimental approach to life. And yet, the couple's music was also accessible to a broader demographic—something that made them even more powerful in the mainstream.

The duo's success reached its peak as they became cultural icons, not just for their music but for their personalities. They represented everything that was both exciting and tumultuous about the 1960s: freedom, rebellion, and the blurring of traditional boundaries. Their success was also a reflection of how the music industry was changing. The 1960s and early 1970s marked a shift away from the more formulaic, traditional pop music of the past toward something more experimental and diverse. Sonny and Cher, with their innovative sound and image, were at the forefront of that change.

But with fame came its own set of challenges. The pressures of being in the public eye, constantly on tour, and dealing with the complexities of their personal relationship took its toll. The demands of their busy schedule, coupled with the strains in their marriage, began to impact their personal and professional lives. The stress of balancing their roles as musicians, entertainers, and a married couple led to cracks in their relationship, but it didn't stop their musical momentum. Even as their personal lives began to unravel, their chart success continued to soar.

Looking back at the Sonny and Cher era, it's clear that their time at the top was much more than just a passing trend. Their music, their image, and their ability to connect with audiences in ways that few others could made them stand out as one of the most memorable duos in the history of pop culture. Their influence, both musically and stylistically, can still be felt today. The tracks they recorded, the fashion they pioneered, and the brand they created continue to inspire artists, entertainers, and fans around the world.

As Sonny and Cher took over the charts, they didn't just shape the sound of their time—they helped define the cultural landscape of the 1960s and beyond. Their music was a voice for the changing times, a reflection of the youthful rebellion and idealism of the era. Even as their careers and personal lives began to take different paths, the legacy of their music and their cultural impact remained indelible. The Sonny and Cher era may have been brief, but it was undeniably powerful.

The Sonny & Cher Comedy Hour

The Sonny & Cher Comedy Hour was more than just a television show—it was a cultural event that encapsulated the spirit of the early 1970s. The show premiered on August 1, 1971, at a time when variety shows were incredibly popular, and it quickly became a hit. Hosted by the dynamic and ever-charismatic duo, Sonny and Cher, the show allowed them to combine their musical talents with their budding comedic chops, creating a unique blend of music, humor, and charm that captivated millions of viewers every week.

The success of the show was a reflection of Sonny and Cher's broad appeal. On one hand, they were pop music stars, known for their chart-topping hits like "I Got You Babe" and "The Beat Goes On." But the show gave them the opportunity to showcase an entirely different side of their personalities. The couple's natural chemistry, paired with their ability to laugh at themselves and their public image, made for an entertaining and highly relatable television experience. While their music had already made them famous, it was the *Sonny & Cher Comedy Hour* that truly made them household names and solidified their place in pop culture history.

From the very first episode, the show was a hit, drawing in millions of viewers. Its blend of comedy sketches, musical performances, and guest appearances made it a must-watch for a wide audience. The format was built around the couple's on-screen chemistry, which was both humorous and heartwarming. Sonny, with his sharp wit and quick sense of humor, played the perfect foil to Cher's sassy, rebellious personality. The playful banter between them was a highlight of every episode, with Sonny often teasing Cher and Cher responding with her trademark deadpan humor. Their ability to play off each other's strengths gave the show a unique charm and kept viewers coming back week after week.

One of the most iconic aspects of the *Sonny & Cher Comedy Hour* was the way it allowed Cher to fully embrace her persona as a style icon. Every episode featured her in a wide array of costumes—many of which became as famous as the show itself. Cher's outfits were often bold, glamorous, and daring, with extravagant hats, feather boas, and glittering gowns that became signature pieces of her fashion legacy. The show was as much about her fashion as it was about the music and comedy, and Cher's on-screen presence was captivating. The way she combined her sharp wit with her stunning appearance made her one of the most influential women on television at the time.

Sonny, too, had his moments in the spotlight, though in a more understated way. His role as the comedic straight man was essential to the show's success. He played the part of the charming, lovable husband to perfection, often engaging in hilarious antics with Cher, all while maintaining his role as the bandleader and the show's anchor. His ability to balance his comedic timing with the occasional heartfelt moment was one of the reasons the show resonated so deeply with audiences.

The comedy sketches were another highlight of the show, with Sonny and Cher taking on a wide variety of roles. Whether they were impersonating famous celebrities, performing slapstick routines, or poking fun at the celebrity culture they were a part of, the sketches offered a lighthearted, often irreverent take on the entertainment world. They weren't afraid to laugh at themselves, and that self-deprecating humor endeared them even more to viewers. This willingness to poke fun at their own public personas—Sonny's attempts to keep things together while Cher stole the show—was a big part of the show's success.

The *Sonny & Cher Comedy Hour* also featured a rotating cast of guest stars, adding another layer of appeal. Celebrities from all walks of life made appearances on the show, adding to its sense of glamour and excitement. Guests included big names like Bob Hope, Tim Conway, and even future stars like Elton John. The wide variety of guests showcased the couple's reach and influence across different sectors of the entertainment industry. The presence of these stars helped bring additional attention to the show and ensured that it remained fresh and relevant.

The show's music segments were also a significant part of its appeal. Cher, ever the performer, would often take center stage to perform her hits, dazzling audiences with her vocal range and stage presence. The musical performances allowed viewers to experience Cher's talents in a way they hadn't before, and they further cemented her status as a multifaceted star. Sonny, too, would perform alongside her, and their on-stage chemistry was palpable. The musical numbers were carefully choreographed and visually engaging, making each one feel like a mini-concert.

However, while the *Sonny & Cher Comedy Hour* was a ratings success and a beloved television staple, it wasn't without its challenges. Behind the scenes, the couple's personal relationship was starting to show signs of strain. The pressure of constantly being in the public eye, managing their individual careers, and maintaining a family life began to take its toll. Tensions between Sonny and Cher were becoming more apparent, and it was clear that their marriage was beginning to unravel. Despite these personal issues, they continued to work together on the show, and their professional commitment to the program never wavered.

In 1974, the *Sonny & Cher Comedy Hour* ended its run, but its impact on pop culture endured. Sonny and Cher's relationship, both on-screen and off, became part of the public consciousness. The show had made them one of the most recognizable couples in America, and even though their personal lives took different paths, their partnership on the show had created a lasting legacy.

The *Sonny & Cher Comedy Hour* was not just a variety show—it was a cultural touchstone. It helped shape the landscape of 1970s television and influenced how future television duos would approach comedy and entertainment. Cher, in particular, emerged from the show as one of the most iconic figures in pop culture. The show allowed her to showcase not only her musical talents but her sense of humor, her style, and her personality in a way that hadn't been seen before. Sonny, too, was able to cement his place in entertainment history, carving out a role as both a performer and a producer.

In the years that followed, both Sonny and Cher would go on to pursue solo careers, but the legacy of their time together on *The Sonny & Cher Comedy Hour* would continue to define their careers. The show not only marked a peak in their professional lives but also made them symbols of the era—a time when entertainment was defined by personality, style, and the chemistry between its stars. For millions of viewers, the show was a weekly ritual that provided laughter, music, and an unforgettable glimpse into the lives of two of the most beloved entertainers of the 1970s.

Behind the Glamour

Behind the glittering facade of fame and fortune, the lives of Sonny and Cher were far from the picture-perfect world they often presented to the public. While they dominated the music charts, entertained millions on television, and set fashion trends that would influence future generations, their personal struggles were equally as complex and challenging. The 1970s, for all their success, were also marked by intense pressure, emotional turmoil, and personal sacrifices that often went unseen by their adoring fans.

As Sonny and Cher's fame grew, so did the demands on their personal lives. The constant public scrutiny, the never-ending work schedule, and the challenges of maintaining a family while navigating the complexities of their careers placed an incredible strain on their relationship. What had once been a fairytale romance between two ambitious young stars soon became a complicated, high-stakes balancing act. While their on-screen chemistry was undeniable, behind closed doors, their marriage began to unravel.

Cher, known for her bold persona and unflinching independence, found herself grappling with the expectations placed upon her, both as a wife and as an entertainer. While she had always been fiercely protective of her individuality, she was increasingly faced with the reality that her career was largely controlled by her husband, Sonny. Sonny, who had a clear vision for their brand and a strong business acumen, made many of the decisions for their professional lives, but this control was not always in alignment with Cher's growing desire for autonomy. She wanted to carve out her own identity, not just as part of the Sonny and Cher duo, but as an individual artist. This tension between their professional partnership and her personal desires would eventually lead to a breaking point.

Their relationship, once marked by playfulness and mutual admiration, began to show signs of wear. The public's obsession with their on-screen personas and their portrayal of a perfect, loving couple became increasingly difficult to maintain in the face of their private struggles. They had built a brand around their relationship, but the cracks that were appearing in their marriage were becoming harder to conceal. Sonny's attempts to control their image and career sometimes clashed with Cher's need for independence, leading to frequent arguments and emotional distance. The pressures of fame, compounded by the relentless expectations of their fans and the media, took a toll on their emotional well-being.

The personal struggles between Sonny and Cher also mirrored the larger cultural shifts of the time. The 1970s were a period of great change, both in the entertainment industry and in society at large. Women, in particular, were asserting their independence and demanding more control over their careers and lives. Cher, with her increasing desire to break free from Sonny's shadow, became a symbol of this growing empowerment. Her fashion choices, her outspoken opinions, and her decisions to take control of her career were a reflection of the broader feminist movement that was gaining momentum. However, navigating this desire for autonomy within the confines of a partnership that was deeply entrenched in both their personal and professional lives was not easy.

Meanwhile, Sonny, who had once been the driving force behind their career, found himself in a difficult position. While his business savvy and commitment to their success were key factors in their rise to fame, he struggled with the shifting dynamics of their relationship. As Cher began to demand more creative freedom and recognition for her individual talents, Sonny felt threatened. This shift in their professional relationship paralleled the emotional distance that was growing between them. While Sonny had always been the more visible figure in their partnership, Cher's increasing confidence and ambition began to take center stage. This change in dynamics, while empowering for Cher, left Sonny feeling less secure and more resentful, contributing to the growing tension between them.

Despite these challenges, the public continued to see the couple as one of the most successful duos in entertainment. Their television show, *The Sonny & Cher Comedy Hour,* was a hit, drawing millions of viewers every week, and their music continued to dominate the charts. But behind the glamour of the stage, the strain of their personal lives was becoming harder to ignore. The demands of their careers and the pressures of fame were creating cracks in their relationship that would eventually lead to their separation.

By 1974, their marriage had reached its breaking point. The couple announced their separation, shocking fans and marking the end of an era for Sonny and Cher. The decision to part ways was not easy, but it was ultimately one that allowed both of them to pursue their individual careers. Cher, who had long been yearning for independence, was finally able to embrace her own artistic vision and take control of her career. Sonny, too, went on to explore new ventures, including a political career, but his professional life was never quite the same without Cher by his side.

Despite their separation, Sonny and Cher remained linked in the public eye. Their shared history, their musical achievements, and their undeniable chemistry kept them connected in the hearts and minds of their fans. Cher's solo career flourished in the years following their divorce, with her transition into film and her eventual resurgence as a pop icon. Her ability to reinvent herself time and time again cemented her place as one of the most resilient and versatile entertainers in the world. Sonny, on the other hand, faced his own set of challenges in the wake of the divorce, but he remained a significant figure in the entertainment world until his untimely death in 1998.

Their separation, though painful, allowed both Sonny and Cher to grow individually and further define their own identities. Cher's success as a solo artist, actress, and fashion icon was a testament to her ability to break free from the expectations that had once bound her. She not only thrived in her personal career but also became an inspiration for women who were seeking to break free from traditional gender roles and assert their independence in the entertainment industry. Cher's ability to reinvent herself, both in her music and in her public image, was nothing short of remarkable. She embraced each new phase of her career with confidence, proving that she could rise above the struggles that once defined her.

For Sonny, the end of his partnership with Cher marked the loss of not only a personal relationship but a professional one as well. While he continued to remain active in the entertainment industry, his post-Sonny & Cher career was never quite as successful as the heyday they had shared. Nonetheless, Sonny remained a beloved figure in American pop culture, remembered not just for his work with Cher but for his contributions to the entertainment world as a whole.

Behind the glamour of their public personas, Sonny and Cher faced struggles that were every bit as complex and human as anyone else. The pressures of fame, the dynamics of their marriage, and the pursuit of their individual dreams led them on divergent paths. Yet, their legacy as one of the most iconic entertainment duos of all time endures. The *Sonny & Cher* era, while short-lived, marked a turning point in the entertainment industry, and their story serves as a reminder of the complexities of fame, love, and personal growth in the face of overwhelming pressure.

4

Breaking Out as a Solo Artist
Finding Her Own Voice

C her once said, "I don't ever want to be a one-hit wonder. I want to be remembered for the longevity of my career." This statement captures the essence of Cher's journey as a solo artist—a journey defined by resilience, reinvention, and the unyielding desire to define herself on her own terms. After parting ways with Sonny, Cher was not just stepping into the unknown; she was stepping into an opportunity to reclaim her voice and carve a path that would solidify her as a force to be reckoned with in the entertainment industry.

The transition from being part of the iconic duo Sonny & Cher to a solo artist was not an easy one. While her music career was always intertwined with Sonny's, Cher's desire to establish her own identity as an individual artist had been simmering beneath the surface for years. She had always been more than just the glamorous partner to Sonny Bono; she was a woman with her own ambitions, dreams, and an unyielding drive to succeed. But leaving behind the comfort and security of their partnership was a daunting task. The world had known her as part of a team, and now she had to prove that she could thrive independently.

In 1975, Cher took the first steps towards finding her own voice as a solo artist, and it wasn't without its challenges. She signed with Warner Bros. Records and began working on her debut solo album. The resulting album, *Stars*, reflected the bold, self-assured persona that Cher was beginning to embrace. It was a departure from the pop sound that had defined her early career, exploring a more soulful and mature direction. However, while the album showcased her versatility as an artist, it didn't exactly meet the commercial success she had hoped for. The music world had shifted since the height of her popularity with Sonny, and Cher, with her unique blend of power and vulnerability, was still finding her place in an increasingly complex music landscape. Yet, despite the album's lukewarm reception, Cher's determination was unwavering. She was not willing to let one setback define her career.

It wasn't long before Cher began to experiment with her sound, taking on new projects that would push her into the mainstream as a solo artist. In 1977, she released *I Paralyze*, a disco-inspired album that marked a clear departure from her previous works. Disco was taking over the charts at the time, and Cher, ever the chameleon, was quick to adapt. The album featured a mix of catchy beats and soulful ballads, with Cher's vocals taking on a new, polished quality. Her ability to blend her raw, emotive delivery with the upbeat, danceable rhythms of disco was a testament to her musical versatility. Yet again, the commercial success was moderate, and Cher realized that she had to go further to break through to a wider audience.

Her turning point came in 1980 with the release of *Believe*, a record that would change the trajectory of her career forever. At the time, Cher was already an established name in pop culture, but *Believe* marked the moment when she solidified herself as not just a music icon, but a cultural one. The title track of the album became an instant hit, topping the charts in multiple countries and showcasing Cher's transformation into a trailblazer in the dance-pop genre. *Believe* is often considered her ultimate reinvention, capturing both her timeless appeal and her ability to evolve with the times. The use of Auto-Tune in the song, which was revolutionary at the time, gave her voice a futuristic, robotic quality that resonated with both old fans and new listeners. The song's success was a defining moment in Cher's career—she had found her own voice, one that resonated with a new generation of fans while maintaining her core essence.

Cher's bold move into dance music in the late '90s was more than just a stylistic choice—it was a reflection of her uncanny ability to stay relevant, no matter the musical climate. When *Believe* hit the airwaves, it wasn't just another pop song; it was a declaration of independence and resilience. Cher had shed the image of the '60s pop starlet, the '70s disco diva, and had emerged as a force within the new millennium. The album's success was global, with *Believe* topping the charts across Europe, Australia, and North America. It was a hit in clubs, on the radio, and in mainstream media. Her voice was unmistakable, her presence was undeniable, and the public had embraced this new chapter of her career with open arms.

The song "Believe" wasn't just a commercial triumph—it was a personal one, too. For Cher, the success of the single and album represented everything she had fought for in her solo career. She had, for all intents and purposes, found her voice. No longer constrained by the expectations of her partnership with Sonny, she was able to express herself freely, both musically and creatively. With this new identity came a sense of empowerment, a realization that she was more than capable of defining her career on her own terms.

This success didn't come by accident. Cher was no longer a young artist searching for a foothold in an unpredictable industry. She had lived through countless ups and downs, each one teaching her valuable lessons about resilience and reinvention. She had seen firsthand the changing tides of the music industry and had, time and again, adapted herself to stay relevant. Cher had embraced the challenges that came with being a solo artist, and with *Believe*, she finally reaped the rewards of her efforts.

Following the success of *Believe*, Cher's career entered another phase of unprecedented success. She embarked on world tours, performing to sold-out arenas and cementing her place as a global superstar. Cher was no longer just a pop star; she had become a cultural icon. She had transcended the boundaries of music and entertainment, becoming a living symbol of reinvention. Her influence was felt not only in the music industry but in fashion, film, and even activism. Cher, once a girl from El Centro, California, was now an international legend, her career a reflection of the limitless possibilities that come with resilience and self-expression.

Cher's journey as a solo artist was not without its setbacks, but it was those very struggles that forged the path to her success. From her early days in the spotlight to her evolution into a solo performer, Cher's story is a testament to her determination, adaptability, and willingness to push the boundaries of her own talent. She didn't just find her voice as a solo artist; she found a way to redefine what it meant to be an icon in the ever-changing landscape of music. Through each reinvention, Cher remained true to herself and her artistry, proving that it's never too late to break free and find the strength to rise above the challenges that life throws your way.

Early Hits and Misses

Cher's early years as a solo artist were filled with both triumphs and struggles, and while she eventually solidified her place as a pop culture icon, it wasn't an easy road to get there. After parting ways with Sonny Bono, Cher had to build her career from the ground up, and that meant facing the harsh realities of the entertainment industry, where success is never guaranteed, and failure is always a possibility.

In 1969, Cher's first real attempt to break out on her own was her album *Sonny & Cher's Greatest Hits*, which featured both her solo work and her songs with Sonny. However, it was clear that Cher was not quite yet her own entity in the eyes of the public. Her reputation as part of the beloved duo still overshadowed her attempts to be seen as an individual artist. That year, she released *Cher*, her first self-titled album, which marked a distinct departure from her work with Sonny. It included a mix of rock, pop, and folk influences, a reflection of her desire to explore new sounds. However, despite Cher's deep passion for the music, the album failed to make a significant impact on the charts.

Her next solo effort came in 1971 with *Gypsys, Tramps & Thieves*. It was a turning point for her as it was a major commercial success. The title track became one of her biggest hits to date, reaching number one on the Billboard Hot 100 and cementing her position as a solo artist. Cher's ability to blend elements of pop with her unique vocal stylings struck a chord with fans, and she was finally starting to shake off the shadow of Sonny. The album itself was a reflection of Cher's growing confidence in her ability to carry her own career. She had found a sound that suited her voice and allowed her to shine, but it was also clear that her journey as a solo artist would require more than just one successful single.

Despite the success of *Gypsys, Tramps & Thieves*, Cher's next few albums saw a decline in commercial success. *Foxes*, her 1973 album, failed to generate the same level of interest, and despite her continued efforts to find a new sound, her solo career wasn't taking off in the way she had hoped. It seemed as though Cher was stuck in a cycle of hits and misses, each album offering a glimpse of her potential but not quite managing to capitalize on her previous success.

The challenges she faced during these years were not just musical. In the early 1970s, Cher was navigating life as a single woman, having divorced Sonny and struggling with her own identity both personally and professionally. Her confidence was shaken at times, especially when she wasn't finding the success she was used to in her joint projects with Sonny. But through it all, Cher's resilience remained unwavering. She continued to tour, write, and record, determined to prove to herself and her fans that she could succeed on her own. It was this determination, this refusal to give up on her dream, that would eventually propel her toward the next chapter of her career.

Cher's early solo career was filled with moments of self-discovery, both in terms of her artistry and her personal life. While the early years brought plenty of challenges, they also shaped the fearless and unapologetic woman she would become. Through the struggles, she learned to trust her instincts, push boundaries, and embrace the idea that she wasn't just a pop singer—she was an artist, capable of tackling whatever musical genre or role came her way.

What truly set Cher apart during this time, however, was her ability to adapt. Where other artists might have fallen into despair or given up after facing a string of commercial failures, Cher used each setback as a lesson. She wasn't interested in being confined to one genre or sound. Instead, she embraced the opportunity to experiment, blending rock, pop, folk, and later, disco into her music. Cher's commitment to reinvention became one of her trademarks, and this approach to her career allowed her to evolve continuously, staying relevant no matter the musical landscape.

While early hits like "Gypsys, Tramps & Thieves" marked a high point in her solo career, the misses were equally as important in shaping her future. It was during these struggles that Cher developed a deep understanding of the importance of perseverance, adaptability, and risk-taking. By the time she reached the late 1970s, her willingness to explore new musical territory, from disco to rock to even experimental sounds, began to pay off. Cher wasn't just trying to find a sound that worked for her—she was determined to forge a legacy that would stand the test of time, proving to herself and the world that she was more than just a fleeting moment in pop history.

As the years passed, Cher's early missteps began to fade into the background. Each failure, each missed opportunity, became an integral part of her story. Her later successes were built on the foundation of those early years, a testament to her determination to make it as a solo artist. Whether it was her ability to reinvent her music or her resilience in the face of setbacks, Cher's early years were integral in shaping the persona that would go on to captivate the world for decades to come.

By the time Cher fully broke out as a solo artist, she had amassed a wealth of experience, had learned the art of reinvention, and had gained the confidence needed to succeed. Her early hits and misses had not only provided her with valuable lessons but also pushed her toward greatness. The rest of her career would prove that even when faced with obstacles and challenges, Cher would always find a way to bounce back, stronger and more determined than before.

Reinventing Herself in the 1970s

The 1970s were a transformative decade for Cher, one that saw her evolve from a successful pop singer to a versatile artist who was unafraid to reinvent herself time and again. While the early part of the decade saw her struggling to establish herself as a solo act, it was also a time when Cher began to embrace new styles, new sounds, and a fresh perspective on her career. It wasn't just her music that changed during this period, but also her public persona. Cher, in the 1970s, would begin to craft the image of the bold, confident, and fearless icon we know today.

After her split from Sonny Bono and the end of their famous partnership, Cher was determined to forge her own path. Yet, in the early years of her solo career, despite releasing albums like *Cher* (1971) and *Gypsys, Tramps & Thieves* (1971), which showcased her undeniable talent, her commercial success was inconsistent. While she had her hits, like the chart-topping single "Gypsys, Tramps & Thieves," she also faced the reality that the public still saw her as part of Sonny & Cher, not as an individual artist in her own right.

But Cher wasn't one to be defined by the past, and she recognized that in order to truly break free and thrive on her own, she needed to reinvent her image and musical style. She had already proven she could sing, but now she was determined to prove she could do more, that she was an artist capable of embracing change and new challenges.

In 1973, Cher took a bold step by embracing the popular sounds of the time: disco and glam rock. She moved away from the traditional pop sound she had been known for and began experimenting with danceable beats, flamboyant fashion, and theatricality. Her appearance began to match her newly adopted style. Gone was the demure, sweet image of the early '60s; Cher now embraced a more daring, edgy look, full of metallics, feathers, and bold statement pieces that made her stand out both musically and visually. This period marked the beginning of her ability to blend fashion, performance, and music into one seamless and memorable persona.

One of the key moments in her 1970s reinvention came with her appearance in the 1974 film *The Witches of Eastwick*, a role that allowed Cher to explore new aspects of her acting ability while also pushing her musical boundaries. It was also during this time that she began to embrace a more deeply personal and introspective approach to her music. This evolution came to fruition with her 1975 album *Stars*, which explored a more soulful sound, fusing elements of rock, disco, and pop into something entirely new and innovative.

The music itself was proof of Cher's versatility—she was no longer bound by the limitations of one genre or sound. "Half-Breed" and "Dark Lady," two standout tracks from her *Stars* album, were not just commercially successful—they were deeply personal, reflecting Cher's own experiences of feeling like an outsider and grappling with her identity. The songs spoke to the woman Cher had become—bold, unapologetic, and completely unafraid to be herself, regardless of what the world thought of her.

While *Stars* was a significant moment in her reinvention, the 1970s also marked a critical shift in her career and her personal life. During this period, she divorced Sonny Bono and moved on from their shared professional career. This time of reinvention wasn't just about the music—it was about Cher's desire to prove that she could stand on her own, away from the shadow of their former partnership. As she transitioned into new phases of both her career and personal life, she was in the midst of redefining what it meant to be an artist in the ever-changing entertainment world.

Her television appearances in the 1970s, including *The Sonny & Cher Comedy Hour* and later *Cher*, the show that she headlined as a solo performer, helped solidify her new image. *Cher* was a platform for the artist to showcase her new persona—an eclectic mix of glam, comedy, and musical experimentation. The show helped her break away from the "Sonny and Cher" era and create an individual identity, one that was both empowering and entertaining. The audience was now seeing her not just as a singer, but as an entertainer in every sense of the word. With these shows, Cher expanded her range, demonstrating her sharp sense of humor, her impeccable comedic timing, and her ability to entertain on every level.

In the midst of her reinvention, Cher also began to push the boundaries of fashion. Her image in the 1970s became synonymous with innovation. She embraced extravagant costumes, often designed by the legendary Bob Mackie, whose creations became iconic in their own right. Cher was no longer just wearing clothes; she was using fashion as a way to make a statement, to express herself, and to shape the way the public viewed her. Her glamorous costumes became part of her signature style, elevating her from a singer to a trendsetter who would inspire countless others in the fashion and entertainment industries.

But it was the music of the late 1970s that truly solidified Cher's reinvention as an artist. By this time, she was no longer afraid to take risks, to try new things, and to embrace whatever was trendy or cutting edge. She explored disco music, a genre that was sweeping the world at the time, with albums like *Take Me Home* (1979). While the album wasn't an instant chart-topper, it signified a crucial part of her evolution. With the release of the album, Cher embraced the energy of the disco movement, fully immersing herself in a genre that had already begun to define the sound of the decade. Cher's ability to stay relevant by embracing these trends set her apart from other artists, proving her resilience and adaptability in the face of a rapidly changing industry.

Though she was largely associated with the glitzy world of disco in the late '70s, Cher's reinvention wasn't limited to the music scene. By the end of the decade, Cher had established herself as a multifaceted artist—a singer, actress, and television personality with a flair for dramatic flair and cultural impact. Her ability to blend different genres of music, styles of performance, and personal aesthetics allowed her to transcend the limitations of a single career path. She was carving out a space for herself in the pop culture zeitgeist, unapologetically paving her own way and creating a lasting legacy in the process.

Cher's reinvention in the 1970s laid the foundation for everything that was to come in the following decades. She had transformed from a talented young woman trying to make her way in the world into a self-assured artist who was confident in her own skin. Cher was no longer the girl who once had to step out of Sonny's shadow; she had fully embraced her own identity, both artistically and personally. This reinvention in the '70s marked the beginning of a new era—one in which Cher would continue to evolve, innovate, and inspire, solidifying her place as one of the most iconic figures in music and entertainment history.

5

The Hollywood Years
A Natural Actress Emerges

"Acting is not about being someone different. It's finding the similarity in what is apparently different, then finding myself in there." This quote by Meryl Streep, one of Hollywood's finest, resonates deeply with Cher's transition from music to acting—a move many believed would be impossible for someone so synonymous with pop stardom. Yet, Cher's entry into Hollywood not only proved the skeptics wrong but also revealed a natural talent that was as raw as it was unexpected. It was the beginning of a new chapter, one that showcased her versatility and sheer determination to excel in yet another domain.

For Cher, the leap into acting was less of a planned career move and more of a challenge she embraced head-on. She didn't set out to become an actress to prove a point, but once the opportunity presented itself, she approached it with the same tenacity and commitment that had characterized her music career. In the early years, Hollywood wasn't particularly kind to musicians who attempted to make the jump to acting. The entertainment industry, often harsh and unforgiving, was quick to pigeonhole artists, doubting their ability to succeed outside their established niches. But Cher was no ordinary artist, and her journey into acting was anything but conventional.

Her first foray into the world of film came in 1967 with *Good Times*, a campy Sonny & Cher vehicle that was intended to capitalize on the duo's growing fame. The film, while playful and lighthearted, didn't exactly showcase Cher's acting potential. Critics dismissed it as fluff, and audiences didn't connect with its quirky humor. While it wasn't the breakout role Cher may have hoped for, it planted a seed of possibility—one that she would revisit years later when the time was right.

By the late 1970s, Cher was ready to take another shot at acting, this time with a more serious approach. She started small, taking acting lessons and immersing herself in the craft. It wasn't enough for her to rely on her charisma or star power; she wanted to understand the art of acting from the inside out. This dedication caught the attention of director Robert Altman, who cast her in his stage production of *Come Back to the Five and Dime, Jimmy Dean,*

Jimmy Dean. Cher's performance was met with critical acclaim, and it marked a turning point in her acting career. She wasn't just a singer dabbling in acting anymore—she was proving herself as a serious actress with depth and range.

The success of the play led to Cher's casting in the 1982 film adaptation of *Come Back to the Five and Dime, Jimmy Dean, Jimmy Dean*, where she reprised her role as Sissy, a woman grappling with her past and her identity. The film showcased Cher in a new light, revealing a vulnerability and complexity that audiences hadn't seen before. Critics took notice, praising her performance and highlighting her ability to convey raw emotion with authenticity. For Cher, it was a moment of validation—a sign that she could hold her own in the highly competitive world of Hollywood.

Following the success of *Jimmy Dean*, Cher's acting career gained momentum. In 1983, she starred in *Silkwood* alongside Meryl Streep and Kurt Russell. Directed by Mike Nichols, the film was a gripping drama based on the true story of Karen Silkwood, a whistleblower in the nuclear industry. Cher played Dolly Pelliker, a lesbian friend and co-worker of Silkwood, in a role that demanded both subtlety and emotional depth. Once again, critics were impressed by Cher's performance, with many noting her ability to disappear into the character and deliver a nuanced portrayal. Her work in *Silkwood* earned her an Academy Award nomination for Best Supporting Actress—a remarkable achievement for someone who had only recently begun to establish herself as a serious actress.

With *Silkwood*, Cher had crossed a major threshold. She was no longer seen as a pop star trying her hand at acting; she was a bona fide actress, respected by her peers and recognized for her talent. This newfound credibility opened the door to more challenging and diverse roles. In 1985, she starred in *Mask*, a drama directed by Peter Bogdanovich, where she played Rusty Dennis, the fiercely protective mother of a boy with a severe facial deformity. The role required Cher to convey both strength and vulnerability, and her performance earned widespread acclaim. Critics lauded her ability to bring authenticity to the character, and the film was a box office success, further solidifying her place in Hollywood.

By this point, Cher had become a force to be reckoned with in the film industry, but she wasn't content to rest on her laurels. She continued to seek out roles that challenged her and allowed her to explore new facets of her talent. In 1987, she starred in two films that would become iconic: *The Witches of Eastwick* and *Moonstruck*. In *The Witches of Eastwick*, Cher played Alexandra Medford, one of three women who unwittingly summon the devil, played by Jack Nicholson. The film was a darkly comedic fantasy that showcased Cher's ability to balance humor and drama with ease.

But it was her role in *Moonstruck* that truly cemented her status as a Hollywood star. In the film, Cher played Loretta Castorini, a widowed bookkeeper who falls in love with her fiancé's brother, played by Nicolas Cage. The romantic comedy, directed by Norman Jewison, was both a critical and commercial success, and Cher's performance was hailed as a career-defining moment. Her portrayal of Loretta was equal parts witty, warm, and poignant, and it earned her the Academy Award for Best Actress in 1988. Accepting the Oscar, Cher stood on stage in a now-iconic black gown, a symbol of her journey from pop star to Hollywood royalty.

Cher's success in Hollywood was a testament to her resilience and determination. She had defied the odds, breaking free from the stereotypes that had once confined her and proving that she was more than capable of excelling in multiple arenas. Her acting career not only added another dimension to her artistic legacy but also inspired countless others to pursue their passions fearlessly, regardless of the challenges they might face.

The Hollywood years were a transformative period for Cher, one that revealed the depth of her talent and the strength of her character. She had reinvented herself yet again, proving that there were no limits to what she could achieve. Her journey from pop star to acclaimed actress was a story of grit, passion, and an unwavering belief in her own potential—a story that continues to inspire and captivate audiences to this day.

Breakout Roles in Silkwood and Mask

Cher's breakout roles in *Silkwood* (1983) and *Mask* (1985) marked a turning point in her career, proving her mettle as a serious actress and silencing critics who doubted her transition from music to acting. These films not only solidified her place in Hollywood but also showcased her ability to portray deeply emotional, complex characters with authenticity and nuance.

Silkwood was Cher's first major step into the world of serious cinema. Directed by Mike Nichols, the film was based on the true story of Karen Silkwood, a whistleblower in the nuclear industry. Cher played Dolly Pelliker, a close friend and coworker of Silkwood, portrayed by Meryl Streep. Dolly was a vulnerable yet resilient character, a lesbian navigating her way through the prejudices of society and her workplace.

Cher's performance was a revelation. She captured Dolly's tenderness, humor, and quiet strength with a depth that surprised both critics and audiences. It was a role that required subtlety and a willingness to explore raw, emotional territory. The result was a portrayal so genuine that it earned Cher her first Academy Award nomination for Best Supporting Actress. The recognition not only validated her as a serious actress but also showcased her ability to share the screen with powerhouse performers like Streep and Kurt Russell without being overshadowed.

Mask, released two years later, further cemented Cher's reputation as a formidable acting talent. Directed by Peter Bogdanovich, the film was based on the real-life story of Rocky Dennis, a teenager with a rare facial deformity. Cher played Rusty Dennis, Rocky's fiercely protective and unconventional mother. The role required Cher to embody both the strength and vulnerability of a mother fighting for her son's right to live a normal life while navigating her own struggles with substance abuse.

In *Mask*, Cher delivered a performance that was raw, heartfelt, and deeply human. She brought Rusty to life with a mix of toughness and tenderness, portraying a woman who was unapologetically herself yet deeply devoted to her son. The chemistry between Cher and Eric Stoltz, who played Rocky, was palpable, and their relationship formed the emotional core of the film. Critics praised Cher's ability to balance Rusty's brash exterior with moments of profound vulnerability, creating a character who was as relatable as she was compelling.

The success of *Mask* demonstrated Cher's ability to tackle challenging roles that required emotional depth and complexity.

It also showcased her range as an actress, proving that she could move seamlessly between different genres and character types. The film's critical and commercial success further solidified her position in Hollywood and earned her the Best Actress award at the Cannes Film Festival.

Together, *Silkwood* and *Mask* established Cher as more than just a pop icon—they made her a respected and accomplished actress. These roles were not merely stepping stones in her acting career; they were transformative moments that redefined how the world saw her. They highlighted her resilience, her dedication to her craft, and her ability to connect with audiences on a deeply emotional level.

These breakout roles were a testament to Cher's belief in herself and her willingness to take risks. They were proof that, with talent and determination, it was possible to transcend the limitations of labels and expectations. And for Cher, they were just the beginning of a journey that would see her become one of the most celebrated and versatile artists of her generation.

Winning an Oscar for Moonstruck

Winning an Oscar for *Moonstruck* in 1988 was not just a career-defining moment for Cher; it was a crowning achievement that solidified her transformation from pop icon to Hollywood royalty.

Her portrayal of Loretta Castorini, a sharp-witted, widowed bookkeeper caught in a whirlwind romance with her fiancé's passionate brother, showcased a side of Cher that audiences and critics hadn't fully appreciated before—her ability to embody a character so relatable and grounded that it resonated universally.

The road to her Academy Award for Best Actress wasn't an overnight success. By the time Cher starred in *Moonstruck*, she had already proven her acting chops with critically acclaimed roles in *Silkwood* and *Mask*. However, *Moonstruck* offered her a unique opportunity to lead a film that combined wit, romance, and charm, set against the vibrant backdrop of a close-knit Italian-American community in Brooklyn. Directed by Norman Jewison and written by John Patrick Shanley, the movie was as much a character study as it was a celebration of love in all its messy, unpredictable glory.

Cher's performance as Loretta was a masterclass in subtlety and authenticity. She captured the essence of a woman who is pragmatic and sensible on the surface but yearning for something more beneath her reserved demeanor. From her dry humor to her understated vulnerability, Cher infused the character with layers of complexity that made Loretta unforgettable. Her chemistry with Nicolas Cage, who played Ronny Cammareri—the brooding, hot-headed baker who becomes the object of her affections—was electric. Their fiery, unpredictable dynamic added a spark to the film that kept audiences enthralled.

One of the most iconic scenes in the movie—when Loretta slaps Ronny and exclaims, "Snap out of it!"—perfectly encapsulates Cher's ability to command a scene with just the right mix of humor and intensity. The line became instantly iconic, a testament to Cher's impeccable comedic timing and her knack for delivering dialogue with a punch. It was moments like these that made Loretta such a memorable character and endeared Cher to both audiences and critics alike.

The success of *Moonstruck* was not limited to Cher's performance. The film itself was a critical and commercial triumph, earning six Academy Award nominations and winning three, including Cher's win for Best Actress. On Oscar night, Cher's victory was not only a personal milestone but also a defining cultural moment. Dressed in an unforgettable black sequin and feathered gown by Bob Mackie, Cher made a statement that was as bold and unapologetic as her career. Her acceptance speech was heartfelt and genuine, reflecting the gratitude and pride of an artist who had fought hard to be recognized for her talent.

Winning the Oscar was a validation of Cher's journey—a journey that defied the odds and broke down barriers. As a woman who had started her career as one-half of a pop duo and faced relentless skepticism about her ability to transition into acting, this achievement was more than just an award. It was proof that talent, determination, and resilience could overcome even the most stubborn stereotypes.

The impact of Cher's win extended far beyond her personal career. It inspired countless artists to embrace reinvention and to pursue their passions fearlessly, regardless of public perception or industry expectations. Cher's victory sent a powerful message: that success is not confined to one field or one role, and that true artistry knows no bounds.

Moonstruck remains a beloved classic, and Cher's performance is still celebrated as one of the finest in cinematic history. Her Oscar win marked a peak in her illustrious career, a moment that encapsulated her evolution as an artist and cemented her legacy as one of Hollywood's most versatile and enduring stars.

6

Reinvention in the 1980s and 1990s

The Queen of Comebacks

"Success is not final, failure is not fatal: It is the courage to continue that counts." While this quote from Winston Churchill wasn't penned with Cher in mind, it captures the essence of her career. By the 1980s, Cher had already accomplished what most could only dream of—she was a global music sensation, a respected actress, and a household name. Yet, for all her triumphs, the path forward wasn't without its challenges. This was the era that would cement her as the Queen of Comebacks, a title she earned not by luck but by sheer determination, reinvention, and an unyielding spirit.

The 1980s marked a turning point in Cher's career. While her successes in the music and film industries had made her a star, the road wasn't always smooth. By the early part of the decade, her music career had lost some of its momentum, and her presence in Hollywood, though respected, faced increasing competition from younger, fresher faces. For many, this would have signaled a slow fade from the spotlight. For Cher, it was the spark of a new beginning.

It started with her music. Cher's foray into rock during this time redefined her sound and image, taking her from pop darling to rock powerhouse. Albums like *Black Rose* (1980), while not commercial juggernauts, showcased a grittier, edgier Cher, unafraid to experiment and push boundaries. Critics began to take notice of her willingness to evolve, and while commercial success didn't come immediately, Cher was laying the groundwork for what would become a monumental shift in her career.

Her personal life, too, became part of her transformation. Having separated from Gregg Allman and stepping out of the shadow of her tumultuous relationships, Cher began to embody a new sense of independence. Her public persona evolved to reflect this, and audiences were drawn to her unapologetic authenticity. She was no longer just the glamorous star from *The Sonny & Cher Comedy Hour*; she was a fiercely independent woman carving out her place in a rapidly changing entertainment landscape.

The mid-to-late 1980s saw Cher make a triumphant return to the charts and the big screen. In 1987, her self-titled album *Cher* marked a musical rebirth, with hits like *I Found Someone* reintroducing her to a new generation of fans. The album's polished production and Cher's powerhouse vocals resonated with audiences, signaling her return to musical relevance. But she didn't stop there. By the end of the decade, her albums *Heart of Stone* (1989) and *Love Hurts* (1991) solidified her status as a force to be reckoned with in the music industry. Songs like *If I Could Turn Back Time* and *Just Like Jesse James* became instant classics, proving that Cher wasn't just surviving—she was thriving.

Meanwhile, her acting career was reaching new heights. Following her Oscar-winning performance in *Moonstruck*, Cher continued to take on roles that showcased her versatility and depth. Films like *The Witches of Eastwick* (1987) and *Mermaids* (1990) demonstrated her ability to balance humor and drama, endearing her to audiences and critics alike. She became one of the few entertainers to successfully maintain dual careers in music and acting, a feat that remains rare even today.

Perhaps what made Cher's reinvention so remarkable was her ability to remain relatable while embracing change. She didn't shy away from bold choices, whether it was her decision to embrace rock music, her daring fashion statements, or her outspoken personality. Cher became a symbol of resilience, proving that reinvention wasn't just about adapting to trends but about staying true to oneself while exploring new horizons.

The 1990s brought further success and another layer to her legacy. Her music continued to evolve, with albums that blended pop and rock influences while showcasing her signature contralto voice. At the same time, her activism and philanthropy began to take center stage. Cher used her platform to advocate for causes close to her heart, including LGBTQ+ rights and HIV/AIDS awareness. Her bold stance on social and political issues resonated with fans, reinforcing her image as an artist who wasn't afraid to stand up for what she believed in.

As the decade came to a close, Cher's career trajectory was nothing short of awe-inspiring. She had not only reclaimed her place in the entertainment industry but also redefined what it meant to be a star. At an age when many women in Hollywood and the music world faced dwindling opportunities, Cher was breaking barriers and proving that talent, hard work, and a fearless attitude could defy the odds.

Her journey through the 1980s and 1990s wasn't just a comeback; it was a reinvention that rewrote the rules of what an entertainer could achieve. Cher didn't just adapt to the changing times—she set the standard for how to thrive in them. Her resilience, creativity, and unrelenting determination made her a cultural icon, and her story continues to inspire those who face their own crossroads. As Cher herself once said, "Until you're ready to look foolish, you'll never have the possibility of being great." That fearless approach to life and art is precisely what made her the Queen of Comebacks and a legend in her own right.

Fashion, Fame, and Fearlessness

Fashion, fame, and fearlessness have always been at the heart of Cher's identity. In the 1980s and 1990s, these elements became the driving forces behind her reinvention, cementing her status as not just a music and acting icon but a bona fide cultural phenomenon. At a time when women in entertainment often faced pressures to conform or fade quietly into the background, Cher doubled down on her individuality, using her bold fashion choices, unabashed pursuit of fame, and unshakable courage to redefine what it meant to be a global star.

Fashion was Cher's most visible tool for self-expression, and she wielded it with unmatched confidence. Partnering with legendary designer Bob Mackie, she created looks that were not just outfits but statements—statements of power, defiance, and an unwavering embrace of her unique identity. From the feathered headdresses to the barely-there gowns adorned with glittering sequins, Cher's wardrobe became synonymous with her fearless personality. The infamous black sheer gown she wore to the 1986

Oscars, complete with a towering feathered headpiece, didn't just turn heads—it became an enduring symbol of her refusal to blend in.

These daring fashion choices weren't just for shock value; they were calculated risks that reflected her artistic vision and defiance of societal norms. Cher once remarked, "I've always taken risks, and I've always been different, and I don't think there's anything wrong with that." For her, fashion was a medium of storytelling, a way to communicate her evolving identity and challenge conventional notions of beauty and femininity. Whether strutting across a stage in leather and fishnets or gracing a red carpet in a shimmering, skin-baring ensemble, Cher transformed herself into a walking work of art.

Fame, for Cher, was never just about the spotlight—it was a platform for reinvention and impact. She didn't merely bask in her celebrity status; she used it to break barriers and push boundaries in an industry that often sought to pigeonhole her. By the 1980s, she had firmly shed the image of "Sonny & Cher," carving out a solo identity that was as multifaceted as it was compelling. Her fame was not without challenges—criticism of her relationships, her bold aesthetic, and even her age constantly followed her—but Cher met each with resilience and wit.

Rather than retreat from public scrutiny, Cher leaned into it, owning her narrative and using it to connect with fans on a deeper level. She was one of the first celebrities to openly speak about issues like plastic surgery, not as a means to apologize but as an act of transparency. Her candor about the pressures of fame and the realities of aging in Hollywood made her relatable even as she remained larger than life. She embodied the duality of being a star who could be admired and emulated, yet still approachable and human.

Fearlessness, however, was the trait that tied it all together. Cher's willingness to take risks—whether in her career, her personal life, or her public persona—was the cornerstone of her enduring success. She tackled criticism head-on, often turning it into fuel for her next achievement. When detractors questioned her acting abilities, she won an Oscar. When others thought her music career had peaked, she delivered chart-topping hits like *If I Could Turn Back Time*. And when society tried to dictate what a woman "of her age" should or shouldn't do, Cher defied expectations with every move she made.

Her fearlessness extended beyond her art. Cher became an outspoken advocate for causes she believed in, using her fame to amplify messages that mattered. Her support for LGBTQ+ rights, long before it became mainstream, and her efforts to raise awareness about HIV/AIDS showcased her commitment to using her platform for more than personal gain. She was unafraid to stand up for what she believed, even if it meant going against the grain. This fearlessness made her a role model not just for her talent but for her courage in living authentically.

As the 1990s came to a close, Cher's fashion, fame, and fearlessness remained as relevant as ever. She had not only redefined her own career but also set a precedent for artists across generations. Her ability to balance spectacle with substance, glamour with grit, and boldness with vulnerability made her a cultural icon whose influence extended far beyond music and film. Cher didn't just embrace reinvention—she mastered it, proving that the true key to longevity in the entertainment industry is not just talent but the courage to be unapologetically yourself.

The Birth of 'Believe' and a New Era of Music

"The Birth of *Believe* wasn't just a song—it was a revolution," Cher once said of the track that redefined her career and cemented her status as a musical innovator. By the late 1990s, Cher was already a living legend, but she was about to enter a completely new phase of her journey, one that would transcend generational boundaries and firmly establish her as a timeless force in the music industry. The release of *Believe* in 1998 was not merely a comeback; it was the birth of a phenomenon that would forever change the sound and direction of pop music.

At the heart of *Believe* was the groundbreaking use of Auto-Tune, a technology that was initially designed to correct pitch imperfections. For Cher, it became an artistic tool to create a distinctive robotic effect that gave the song its iconic sound. The decision wasn't without risk—her team initially questioned whether the effect would be too unconventional for mainstream audiences. But Cher, as always, trusted her instincts. The bold choice paid off in ways no one could have predicted.

Upon its release, *Believe* skyrocketed to the top of the charts worldwide, reaching number one in over 20 countries. It became the anthem of the late 1990s, a song that resonated with listeners across all age groups. With its infectious beat, empowering lyrics, and Cher's unmistakable vocal delivery, *Believe* captured the essence of resilience and reinvention. The track earned Cher her first Grammy Award for Best Dance Recording and became the highest-selling single of her career.

The success of *Believe* marked the beginning of a new era, both for Cher and for pop music. It wasn't just the song's popularity that made headlines—it was the way it redefined the industry's perception of aging artists. At 52, Cher became the oldest female solo artist to top the Billboard Hot 100, shattering stereotypes about what women could achieve in the music world. Her success wasn't just a personal triumph; it was a statement to the industry that talent and relevance had no expiration date.

The album that followed, also titled *Believe*, was an equally stunning success. It blended dance-pop with elements of electronica, appealing to a younger audience while still satisfying her longtime fans. Songs like *Strong Enough* and *All or Nothing* showcased Cher's ability to adapt to contemporary trends without losing her signature sound. The album's commercial and critical acclaim cemented her place in music history as a pioneer who wasn't afraid to take risks.

Beyond its sonic impact, *Believe* also symbolized Cher's enduring spirit. The lyrics, brimming with themes of self-empowerment and moving on, resonated deeply with fans who saw in Cher a reflection of their own struggles and triumphs. Lines like *"Do you believe in life after love?"* became anthems of resilience, echoing Cher's personal journey of overcoming obstacles and continuously reinventing herself.

The accompanying tour, *The Do You Believe? Tour*, was another milestone in Cher's career. Known for her theatrical performances and dazzling costumes, Cher delivered a show that was both visually stunning and emotionally engaging. The tour sold out arenas across the globe, proving that her appeal was as strong as ever. Fans flocked to see the icon who had not only reinvented herself musically but also redefined what it meant to be a performer in the modern era.

Critics hailed Cher's transformation as nothing short of revolutionary. While some initially dismissed the Auto-Tune effect as a gimmick, it quickly became clear that *Believe* was far more than a passing trend. The song's influence could be felt across the music industry, inspiring countless artists to experiment with electronic production and vocal effects. From Daft Punk to Kanye West, the ripple effects of Cher's innovation are still evident in today's music landscape.

Cher's embrace of technology didn't just breathe new life into her career—it changed the way music was created and consumed. Her fearless approach to reinvention, combined with her ability to stay ahead of trends, set a new standard for artists striving to remain relevant in an ever-changing industry. She didn't just adapt to the times; she shaped them, proving once again why she was more than just a performer—she was a visionary.

As the 1990s transitioned into the 2000s, the legacy of *Believe* continued to grow. It became a cultural touchstone, a song synonymous with empowerment and reinvention. For Cher, it was a defining moment in a career already filled with extraordinary achievements. It was the ultimate proof that staying true to one's artistry while embracing innovation could lead to unprecedented success.

The birth of *Believe* wasn't just a chapter in Cher's story; it was the beginning of a new book—one that celebrated her status as a pioneer, a legend, and an artist who would never stop pushing boundaries. In the years that followed, Cher continued to build on the foundation *Believe* had laid, but its impact remains unmatched—a shining example of what can be achieved when boldness and creativity collide.

7

A Voice for Change

Advocating for LGBTQ+ Rights

"Until you can look at someone and see the humanity in them, you haven't truly lived." Cher's words echo the passion and determination that have defined her decades-long advocacy for LGBTQ+ rights. Long before it became fashionable for celebrities to champion social causes, Cher was standing up for the LGBTQ+ community—not because it was trendy, but because it was personal. Her journey as an advocate was shaped by love, understanding, and a deep commitment to fairness, and it transformed her into one of the most iconic allies in modern history.

The roots of Cher's connection to the LGBTQ+ community run deep. Her larger-than-life persona, bold fashion choices, and fearless defiance of societal norms made her a natural icon for those who often found themselves on the margins of society. Yet, her advocacy wasn't simply a product of her celebrity—it was grounded in empathy and real-life experiences. When Cher's own child, Chaz Bono, came out as transgender, her role as a mother collided with her role as a public figure. This intersection shaped her approach to advocacy, as she learned firsthand the importance of acceptance, education, and unwavering support.

Cher's initial reaction to Chaz's coming out, however, wasn't without its challenges. Like many parents, she had questions, fears, and a period of adjustment. But instead of allowing those emotions to create distance, Cher leaned into the experience, seeking to understand and grow. She became a vocal supporter of Chaz's journey, using her platform to highlight the struggles and triumphs of the transgender community. Her openness about her own learning process resonated with parents around the world, offering a model of unconditional love and support.

As Cher's public profile grew, so too did her influence within the LGBTQ+ community. In the 1970s and 1980s, when homophobia was rampant and the AIDS epidemic ravaged countless lives, Cher didn't shy away from aligning herself with the fight for equality. She performed at benefits, raised funds for AIDS research, and lent her voice to a movement that desperately needed allies. Her willingness to stand beside the LGBTQ+ community during its darkest hours wasn't just courageous—it was transformative.

One of the defining moments in Cher's advocacy came when she publicly embraced her role as a gay icon. Her music, particularly dance hits like *Believe*, became anthems in LGBTQ+ clubs around the world. These songs weren't just catchy—they were liberating, offering a soundtrack for self-expression and resilience. Cher's concerts became safe spaces where people could be unapologetically themselves, and her acknowledgment of this connection only deepened the bond she shared with her LGBTQ+ fans.

Cher's advocacy extended beyond symbolic gestures; she was committed to real change. Over the years, she has been an outspoken supporter of marriage equality, anti-discrimination laws, and transgender rights. Her voice, amplified by her global fame, brought attention to issues that were often ignored or misunderstood. She didn't just show up for the photo ops—she showed up for the hard conversations, the legislative battles, and the moments of solidarity that truly mattered.

Cher's influence wasn't limited to her activism; it also permeated her artistry. Through her roles in films like *Moonstruck* and *Burlesque*, Cher celebrated individuality and the power of embracing one's true self. These themes resonated deeply with LGBTQ+ audiences, who saw in her performances a reflection of their own struggles and triumphs. Her ability to connect with people through her art was another testament to her authenticity and her unwavering support for the community.

The impact of Cher's advocacy is immeasurable, but its legacy is undeniable. She has inspired countless individuals to live their truth, fight for their rights, and demand respect in a world that often seeks to diminish them. For many, Cher isn't just a celebrity—she's a beacon of hope, a reminder that change is possible, and a testament to the power of love and acceptance.

In a world where celebrities often align themselves with causes for the sake of publicity, Cher's advocacy stands out as genuine, heartfelt, and deeply personal. She didn't step into the role of an LGBTQ+ ally for applause or accolades—she did it because she believed in the humanity and dignity of every person. This authenticity has made her not just an ally but a legend, one whose influence transcends generations and continues to shape the fight for equality.

Even as the world evolves and progress is made, Cher's voice remains as vital as ever. She continues to speak out against injustice, challenge prejudice, and uplift those who need it most. Her advocacy is a reminder that the fight for equality is far from over and that true change requires courage, compassion, and a willingness to stand up for what is right.

For Cher, being a voice for change has never been about seeking recognition—it's about making a difference. And in the hearts of the LGBTQ+ community, she has done just that, becoming a symbol of resilience, love, and unwavering support. Her journey as an advocate is a powerful testament to the idea that when you use your platform for good, you can change the world.

Humanitarian Work and Philanthropy

Cher's commitment to making the world a better place extends far beyond her career in entertainment. While she has long been celebrated as a music and film icon, her role as a humanitarian and philanthropist has equally defined her legacy. Through tireless advocacy, generous contributions, and an unyielding desire to help those in need, Cher has proven that her influence isn't confined to stages or screens—it's deeply embedded in the lives of countless individuals and communities worldwide.

Her humanitarian work began early in her career, driven by a strong sense of empathy and responsibility. Cher has always been vocal about her belief that success comes with an obligation to give back. Over the decades, she has supported causes that span a broad spectrum, from children's welfare and veterans' rights to environmental preservation and animal advocacy. Her approach to philanthropy has been hands-on, passionate, and often personal, reflecting her desire to make a tangible difference in the world.

One of Cher's most notable philanthropic efforts has been her work with children. She has supported numerous organizations dedicated to improving the lives of disadvantaged youth, providing funding for education, healthcare, and recreational programs. Cher has often spoken about the importance of giving children a chance to thrive, believing that nurturing the next generation is key to building a better future.

In addition to her work with children, Cher has also been a fierce advocate for veterans. Deeply moved by the sacrifices made by those in the armed forces, she has worked tirelessly to provide support for wounded soldiers and their families. Her contributions have ranged from funding medical treatments and rehabilitation programs to raising awareness about the challenges faced by veterans after returning home. Her dedication to this cause has earned her widespread respect, both within the military community and beyond.

Cher's compassion extends to the environment, where she has been an outspoken advocate for preserving the planet. From campaigning against deforestation to supporting clean energy initiatives, she has used her platform to draw attention to critical environmental issues. Her activism is not limited to raising awareness; Cher has actively funded conservation projects and worked with organizations dedicated to protecting endangered species and natural habitats.

Animal welfare is another cause close to Cher's heart. She has supported numerous animal rights organizations, advocating for the ethical treatment of animals and working to end practices such as animal testing and poaching. Cher's love for animals is evident in her personal life as well, where she has often shared her home with rescued pets.

Perhaps one of the most impactful aspects of Cher's humanitarian work has been her response to global crises. Whether it's natural disasters, humanitarian emergencies, or social injustices, Cher has consistently stepped up to provide aid and amplify the voices of those affected. For instance, she played a significant role in raising funds and awareness during the AIDS epidemic, supporting both research efforts and programs aimed at helping those living with the disease. Her contributions during this time were critical in combating stigma and providing hope to those affected.

In recent years, Cher's philanthropic efforts have extended to addressing systemic issues such as poverty and inequality. She has funded housing projects, donated to food banks, and supported initiatives aimed at empowering marginalized communities. Her approach to these issues reflects her belief in addressing root causes rather than simply alleviating symptoms, a philosophy that has guided much of her work.

One of the defining traits of Cher's humanitarian efforts is her willingness to stand up for what she believes in, even when it's controversial or unpopular. She has never hesitated to use her voice and resources to challenge injustice, whether it's speaking out against discrimination, advocating for LGBTQ+ rights, or calling attention to global human rights violations. Her courage and conviction have inspired countless others to join her in the fight for a more equitable world.

What sets Cher apart as a philanthropist is not just the scope of her contributions but the depth of her commitment. She doesn't merely lend her name to causes; she immerses herself in the work, often engaging directly with the communities she seeks to help. This hands-on approach has earned her the admiration of both beneficiaries and fellow advocates, solidifying her reputation as a compassionate and dedicated humanitarian.

Cher's philanthropy is not about seeking recognition or accolades—it's about making a difference. Her actions are rooted in a genuine desire to improve the lives of others and leave the world better than she found it. For Cher, giving back is not just an obligation but a calling, one that she has embraced with unparalleled passion and determination.

Through her humanitarian work and philanthropy, Cher has shown that true greatness is measured not by fame or fortune but by the impact one has on others. Her legacy as a humanitarian is as enduring as her contributions to music and film, a testament to her belief in the power of compassion and the importance of using one's influence for good. In a world that often feels divided, Cher's unwavering commitment to kindness and generosity serves as a powerful reminder of what it means to be truly human.

Speaking Out in a Changing World

Cher's role as a public figure has always been more than just about her music and films—she has consistently used her platform to speak out on pressing social issues, shaping the way we think about politics, equality, and the state of the world. In a world that's constantly evolving, Cher has remained a steadfast voice for the marginalized, the oppressed, and the voiceless. Whether it's speaking out against injustice, advocating for equality, or challenging the status quo, she has always been unapologetically vocal, refusing to shy away from controversial topics.

From her early days in the spotlight, Cher made it clear that she wasn't just here to entertain; she was here to make a difference.

Her willingness to tackle hard-hitting issues, sometimes at the risk of public backlash, has become one of her defining characteristics. In an era where celebrities often toe the line for fear of alienating their fanbase, Cher has stood firm in her convictions, never afraid to call out injustice when she sees it.

One of the most notable ways Cher has spoken out is through her outspoken support for women's rights. As a trailblazer in the entertainment industry, she has always advocated for women's equality, both in her career and in her activism. In the 1960s and 1970s, when the feminist movement was gaining momentum, Cher was at the forefront, using her platform to challenge societal norms and push for greater representation of women in media. Her bold choices in fashion, music, and public appearances were not just acts of self-expression but statements about the freedom women should have to define themselves on their own terms.

Her vocal support for the LGBTQ+ community is another powerful example of her speaking out in a changing world. From her early advocacy during the AIDS crisis to her continued efforts to promote LGBTQ+ rights, Cher has long been a fierce ally for those whose rights have been overlooked or denied. She has used her fame to draw attention to issues such as marriage equality, transgender rights, and the fight against discrimination, always putting the voices of the LGBTQ+ community at the forefront. For Cher, this advocacy isn't just about supporting a cause; it's deeply personal, as she has been a mother to a transgender child, and her understanding of the challenges faced by LGBTQ+ individuals is both profound and rooted in love.

Cher's political activism has also been a significant aspect of her speaking out in the modern world. Throughout her career, she has been unapologetically outspoken about her political views, never shying away from expressing her opinions on issues ranging from human rights to climate change. She has used her platform to call out government leaders and hold them accountable for their actions, particularly when it comes to policies that undermine the rights and dignity of vulnerable populations. Cher has consistently used her fame to push for positive change, often using social media as a tool to voice her concerns and rally her fans to take action.

What's remarkable about Cher's approach to speaking out is that she has always been able to balance her advocacy with an ability to connect with people from all walks of life. Her message of acceptance, love, and equality resonates with a wide audience, whether they share her views or not. Cher's ability to bridge divides and open up conversations about difficult topics has made her an enduring figure in the world of activism, one whose impact extends far beyond the entertainment industry.

Cher's activism has also included a deep commitment to racial and social justice. As a strong voice against racism, she has used her influence to call attention to the systemic inequalities that persist in society, whether they affect communities of color or other marginalized groups. Whether she's addressing police brutality, advocating for fair wages, or supporting efforts to reform the criminal justice system, Cher has always remained on the side of those fighting for equality and fairness. Her unwavering commitment to racial justice has earned her respect from activists and ordinary people alike, and she has worked tirelessly to amplify the voices of those affected by injustice.

Cher has also been an outspoken advocate for global causes. Her international humanitarian work has seen her take a stand on everything from global poverty to environmental issues, often working with organizations dedicated to bringing about lasting change in developing countries. She has raised millions for causes such as AIDS research, disaster relief efforts, and global health initiatives, and has consistently used her fame to draw attention to the plight of those in need. Her global reach has allowed her to raise awareness and inspire action on a scale few others could achieve.

Despite facing backlash from critics, especially during times when her views were not as widely accepted, Cher has remained a force of nature in the world of activism. She has faced accusations of being too outspoken, too radical, or too controversial. But these criticisms have never deterred her. Instead, they've only fueled her desire to continue speaking out, no matter the cost. Cher's resilience in the face of adversity has made her a role model for others, showing that it is possible to be true to oneself and one's beliefs, even when the world is pushing back.

Today, Cher's voice continues to be a powerful tool for social change. She speaks out on issues that affect the world's most vulnerable populations, whether it's refugees fleeing war, women fighting for their rights, or communities dealing with the consequences of climate change. She has never stopped using her platform to advocate for those in need, and her activism remains as relevant today as it ever was.

Through her boldness, courage, and determination, Cher has shown us that speaking out in a changing world is not just about offering opinions—it's about taking action, challenging the norm, and making a tangible difference in the lives of others. As she continues to champion causes close to her heart, her example reminds us all of the power one voice can have in shaping the future. Cher's legacy as a speaker of truth and justice will undoubtedly inspire generations to come, proving that when we speak up for what's right, we can change the world.

8

Cher the Icon

Her Influence on Fashion and Style

Cher's influence on fashion and style is nothing short of legendary. She has long been a figure who defies convention, constantly pushing boundaries and redefining what it means to be fashionable. From her early days as a singer to her role as a Hollywood star and beyond, Cher has always had an innate understanding of the power of clothing and appearance, using her outfits as a means of self-expression, empowerment, and cultural influence. It's no exaggeration to say that Cher's style has played a pivotal role in shaping the fashion landscape, making her one of the most iconic style icons of the 20th and 21st centuries.

Her approach to fashion has always been fearless, unafraid to embrace bold, daring choices that others might shy away from.

Whether she was wearing a flowing, bohemian-style gown in the '60s or strutting down the red carpet in a show-stopping Bob Mackie creation, Cher has never been afraid to take risks. What's so remarkable about her style is not just the variety of looks she has embraced over the decades, but the consistency with which she has defined her own narrative through fashion. Cher doesn't just wear clothes—she transforms them into statements, making them an integral part of her identity.

Cher's style in the '60s and '70s was defined by an eclectic, bohemian aesthetic. She became known for her long, flowing hair, dramatic eye makeup, and free-spirited, hippy-inspired outfits. Her early wardrobe choices were a mix of opulent and earthy, often featuring wide-brimmed hats, oversized sunglasses, and long skirts paired with chunky jewelry. This look perfectly suited the times, as it reflected the counterculture movement of the 1960s while maintaining an aura of glamour and mystique. Cher was a figure who both celebrated individuality and embodied the carefree spirit of the era, and her fashion choices reflected that perfectly.

But it was in the early 1970s, as she solidified her position as a pop culture icon, that Cher began to collaborate with fashion designer Bob Mackie, an iconic partnership that would go on to define many of her most memorable looks. Mackie's designs for Cher were nothing short of revolutionary, combining the glamour of Hollywood with a daring, provocative edge. The sequined bodysuits, elaborate headdresses, and skin-baring gowns that Cher wore on stage and at public events became her signature, representing both her personal style and her ability to captivate the world's attention. These pieces were a stark departure from the more conventional fashion choices of the time, and their boldness perfectly matched Cher's personality—confident, assertive, and unapologetically unique.

Cher's outfits often had a theatrical quality, transforming her into a living, breathing work of art. It wasn't just about the clothes themselves, but the way she wore them. Cher carried each piece with a sense of pride, owning every outfit and making it hers. She didn't just wear fashion; she embodied it, bringing her own sense of power and identity into every ensemble. Her outfits told a story, whether it was a glamorous, sparkling gown or a leather ensemble that exuded rock-and-roll coolness. Every outfit was a reflection of the woman she was at that moment—dynamic, evolving, and unafraid to take center stage.

One of the most famous and influential aspects of Cher's style was her mastery of accessorizing. Whether it was through dramatic statement jewelry, feathered boas, or bold hats, she knew how to complete a look with the perfect finishing touch. Her accessorizing often went hand-in-hand with her ability to create a complete persona with her outfits. For Cher, fashion was not just about putting clothes together—it was about telling a story, creating an image that would remain etched in the public's memory.

As the decades progressed, Cher's style evolved with the times, but her ability to turn heads with her fashion choices never waned. In the 1980s, she embraced a more sophisticated, polished look, favoring sleek silhouettes and powerful tailoring. However, even as her style became more refined, she never lost her flair for drama and boldness. Whether she was wearing a tailored black suit with statement earrings or a glittering gown at the Oscars, Cher continued to captivate audiences with her fashion choices.

Her appearance at the 1986 Academy Awards, in which she wore a black, off-the-shoulder Bob Mackie gown adorned with sheer panels and beaded details, is still remembered as one of the most iconic red carpet looks of all time. This moment marked a pivotal point in her evolution as a style icon—she had gone from a rock and roll glamour girl to a refined Hollywood goddess, and yet she still possessed the same fearless approach to fashion that had made her famous in the first place.

In the 1990s, Cher continued to prove that she was a force to be reckoned with when it came to fashion. Her looks in this era were a blend of edgy, rock-chic glam and elegant sophistication, once again showing her versatility as a style icon. Whether it was a leather mini skirt and thigh-high boots or a sleek, figure-hugging dress, Cher was still setting trends and pushing boundaries in her own unique way. She also embraced the world of high fashion in the '90s, attending runway shows and sporting cutting-edge designs from top designers.

In the 2000s and beyond, Cher's influence on fashion remained as strong as ever. Even as trends changed and new fashion icons emerged, Cher continued to inspire designers, stylists, and fans alike. Her ability to mix classic elegance with avant-garde experimentation kept her ahead of the curve, solidifying her reputation as a trendsetter for generations to come. Cher's influence on the fashion world wasn't just about what she wore—it was about the way she wore it. She had an unparalleled ability to command attention and create iconic looks that would be remembered for years to come.

Throughout her career, Cher's style was more than just a reflection of fashion trends; it was a tool for self-expression, a way to communicate who she was at any given moment. Cher was always ahead of her time, anticipating the trends that would emerge in the coming decades and influencing the way fashion evolved. She wasn't just a passive participant in the world of fashion; she was an active creator, shaping her own image and inspiring others to do the same.

Cher's influence on fashion extends far beyond the clothes she wore. She revolutionized the way women thought about their appearance, empowering them to embrace their individuality, take risks, and express themselves without fear of judgment. Cher showed the world that fashion isn't about fitting into a mold; it's about creating your own. Her legacy as a fashion icon continues to inspire not only those who admire her but also the countless designers, stylists, and artists who continue to draw inspiration from her fearless approach to style. Cher's impact on fashion is undeniable, and her ability to transform the way we think about clothes, beauty, and self-expression remains as relevant today as it was when she first rose to fame.

Staying Relevant Through Decades

Cher's ability to stay relevant through decades of ever-changing cultural and musical landscapes is a testament to her unparalleled versatility and relentless drive. Few artists have managed to maintain such a lasting presence in the public eye, but Cher has done so not just by adapting to the times, but by continuously reshaping herself to remain ahead of trends while remaining authentically true to who she is. Her journey is a masterclass in reinvention, one that has made her not just an icon of a particular era, but a constant force in music, fashion, and pop culture.

In the 1960s and 1970s, Cher emerged as a groundbreaking figure in the music world, a solo artist who stood out in a sea of male-dominated charts, first paired with Sonny Bono and later as a solo sensation. Her early career was marked by her distinct voice and magnetic presence, propelling her to the top of the charts. As the music scene evolved and disco dominated the late 1970s, Cher's sound shifted. But rather than fading into the background, she embraced the disco wave and made it her own with songs like "Take Me Home" that showcased her adaptability. Even when trends seemed to be leaving her behind, Cher never wavered. Instead, she carefully honed her craft and reinvented her sound, setting herself up for success in the coming decades.

In the 1980s, when many of her contemporaries from the 1960s and 1970s were starting to fade from the public consciousness, Cher reinvented herself yet again, becoming not only a staple in the world of music but also establishing herself as a force in Hollywood. While many of her contemporaries struggled to stay relevant, Cher seamlessly transitioned from pop star to actress, earning an Academy Award for her performance in *Moonstruck* (1987). It wasn't just her acting that kept her in the spotlight, but her fearlessness in choosing roles that pushed boundaries. She portrayed strong, complex women in *Silkwood* and *Mask*, proving her versatility as an actress, something that many other pop stars of her era failed to achieve.

But Cher's ability to remain relevant is not solely about her acting career. It is, in part, her innate understanding of the intersection between image and music. As pop culture moved into the 1990s, Cher kept her finger on the pulse of emerging trends while continuing to create music that resonated with fans old and new. In 1998, she made one of her most iconic comebacks with the release of *Believe*, an album that marked a major shift in her sound. The title track, with its groundbreaking use of auto-tune, not only became a global hit but also solidified Cher's place in the new wave of pop music, embracing technology while keeping her signature vocal style intact. She had once again proven her ability to remain ahead of the curve, a feat that few artists could match.

The *Believe* album wasn't just a commercial success; it also marked the beginning of a cultural renaissance for Cher. Her ability to merge her old-school glam with cutting-edge production made her relevant to younger audiences while remaining beloved by her longtime fans. The track "Strong Enough" became an anthem of empowerment, and Cher was suddenly at the center of a new generation's musical consciousness. She wasn't just an icon from the past; she was a voice of empowerment for young women and a cultural figure who shaped the direction of the pop world in the late 1990s.

As the 21st century progressed, Cher didn't rest on her laurels. Her relevance continued into the 2000s with her record-breaking

Farewell Tour, a tour that spanned multiple continents and grossed over $250 million, further cementing her status as one of the highest-grossing touring acts of all time. What set Cher apart from other artists embarking on "farewell" tours was that hers wasn't just a final goodbye; it was a celebration of her longevity and relevance. She had become a living legend who defied expectations and delivered a performance that felt fresh and exciting even after decades of fame.

What truly sets Cher apart from other entertainers who have had long careers is her ability to stay relevant while continually evolving her public persona. Cher has never been content to rest on her past achievements. Whether it's releasing new music, starring in hit movies, or using social media to interact with fans, she knows how to stay in the public eye. Her willingness to experiment, take risks, and reinvent herself ensures that she never becomes stale or predictable.

In recent years, Cher has embraced a new generation of fans, both through her activism and her embrace of digital platforms. She has been unafraid to speak out on political issues and social justice causes, especially when it comes to LGBTQ+ rights. Her activism has earned her even more respect, as younger generations look to her as a role model who has consistently used her platform to advocate for marginalized groups. Cher's influence extends far beyond music and fashion—she has used her voice for change in a world that is constantly shifting, ensuring that her relevance endures in ways that are meaningful and impactful.

Social media has also played a crucial role in maintaining Cher's cultural relevance. While some older celebrities may have struggled to transition into the digital age, Cher has embraced platforms like Twitter and Instagram with humor and grace, using them to connect with her global fan base. She has become a meme sensation, known for her witty remarks and sharp commentary, keeping her voice alive in a fast-moving digital age.

Through it all, Cher has remained an enigma, a figure whose public persona never grows old. From her ever-changing fashion choices to her ability to make music that connects with people across generations, Cher has built a career that stands as a beacon of reinvention. She has never been afraid of change, and it is this fearlessness that has allowed her to maintain relevance in an industry that often values youth over experience.

Her career continues to inspire new generations of artists, musicians, and fans who see in her a model of longevity and resilience. Cher's relevance is not just about the clothes she wears or the music she creates—it's about her ability to stay true to herself, to evolve while maintaining the essence of who she is. In a world where trends come and go, Cher is a reminder that staying true to your authentic self is the key to lasting influence. She has shown that reinvention is not only possible—it's necessary for survival. Her legacy continues to shine brightly, influencing the worlds of fashion, music, and culture for years to come.

Inspiring a New Generation

Cher's ability to inspire a new generation of fans is a testament to her exceptional staying power and the depth of her cultural impact. What sets her apart from many other iconic figures is her understanding of the value of adaptability, both in her art and in her approach to life. Whether through her bold fashion choices, fearless performances, or activism, Cher has continually proven that age is merely a number and that reinvention, authenticity, and passion are timeless qualities that can resonate across generations.

As the years have passed, Cher's influence has grown beyond her music and acting career. The younger generations, especially millennials and Gen Z, have embraced her not just as a musical legend but as a pop culture phenomenon. She has become a symbol of strength, independence, and unapologetic authenticity. Cher's message is clear: you can be whoever you want to be, no matter your age, gender, or background. Her willingness to express herself openly and authentically—whether through her powerful performances or bold political stances—has earned her the admiration of young people who see her as a role model.

One of the reasons Cher remains so relevant to newer generations is her ability to adapt to changing times while staying true to her roots. While many artists of her era may have found it difficult to evolve in the ever-changing landscape of pop culture, Cher has embraced it with grace. She's always been one step ahead of trends, whether in music, fashion, or her online presence. Her Twitter and Instagram accounts, where she engages directly with her fans, are filled with witty one-liners, political commentary, and empowering messages. This connection with her fans, particularly the younger ones, has made her a fixture in social media culture, allowing her to transcend the typical boundaries of celebrity and become an authentic, relatable presence in the lives of millions of people.

Cher's fashion sense has also been a major influence on younger generations, who see her as a trailblazer in both the music and fashion industries. Her bold outfits, iconic costumes, and ever-changing hairstyles are often seen as expressions of confidence and individuality. Young fans look to her for inspiration, not just in terms of how they dress, but in how they present themselves to the world. Cher's style is a reminder that fashion is not just about clothes—it's about making a statement, embracing who you are, and refusing to conform to society's expectations.

But it's not just Cher's iconic fashion or catchy pop hits that inspire. Her personal story of reinvention, resilience, and overcoming obstacles resonates deeply with younger people navigating a world filled with uncertainty. Cher has had her fair share of struggles—both public and private—and her ability to rise above them and continue to thrive serves as a source of motivation for anyone facing their own challenges. Whether it's overcoming a difficult childhood, navigating the complexities of marriage and motherhood, or dealing with public scrutiny, Cher has shown that it's possible to overcome adversity and come out stronger on the other side.

Her advocacy work has also played a crucial role in inspiring younger generations. Cher has been an outspoken supporter of LGBTQ+ rights, using her platform to push for social justice and equality. For many LGBTQ+ youth, Cher is not just an artist to admire; she's an ally, someone who has consistently used her voice to advocate for their rights and visibility. Her activism extends beyond just the LGBTQ+ community, as she's also been involved in numerous humanitarian causes, from supporting women's rights to promoting environmental sustainability. These efforts have earned her the respect of young people who value authenticity and activism.

Cher's embrace of new technologies has also made her a modern-day icon to younger generations. Unlike many of her contemporaries who have struggled to adapt to the digital age, Cher has fully embraced it. Her social media presence is filled with moments of humor, wisdom, and even occasional political rants that reflect her desire to engage with her fans on a personal level. The meme culture surrounding her, particularly on Twitter, has only amplified her status as a cultural force. She understands the importance of staying connected with her fans and knows how to use new media to continue her legacy of empowering others.

Perhaps most importantly, Cher has shown that it's never too late to reinvent yourself. She's lived through countless reinventions, from her early days as part of Sonny & Cher, to her solo career, her Hollywood years, and her return to the music scene with the groundbreaking album *Believe*. Every time she has reinvented herself, it's been on her own terms, and this refusal to be defined by a particular era or style has made her a true inspiration to those who might feel like they are too old, too young, or too out of place to make a change in their own lives. Cher's legacy is built on the idea that there are no limits to what you can do if you stay true to yourself and embrace the endless possibilities of reinvention.

In a world that often prioritizes youth and beauty, Cher has remained a figure of empowerment for those who don't fit conventional molds. She is proof that success is not determined by age, appearance, or any other superficial factor. Her fans, particularly young ones, look to her as a symbol of confidence and resilience. Through her example, Cher has shown that you can achieve anything if you are willing to embrace your true self, take risks, and keep going despite the obstacles you may face.

Cher's cultural impact isn't confined to any one decade or generation. She has transcended time, continually inspiring new generations of fans while also remaining deeply connected to the ones who have followed her throughout her career. Her ability to evolve with the times, coupled with her authentic, unapologetic personality, makes her an icon who will continue to influence generations to come. Cher is more than just an entertainer—she is a living testament to the power of self-expression, resilience, and reinvention.

Love and Family
Marriages and Relationships

Cher's personal life, filled with love, loss, and the complexities of relationships, is as captivating as her storied career. Throughout her decades in the limelight, Cher has been open about her experiences with marriage and love, each relationship revealing different facets of her character and evolving sense of self. Despite being surrounded by fame, wealth, and adoration from millions, Cher has always maintained that her relationships, both romantic and familial, were some of the most important aspects of her life.

Her first marriage to Sonny Bono, the man who would help launch her career, remains one of the most talked-about partnerships in pop culture history. The two met in 1962, when Cher was just 16 years old, and Sonny, a struggling musician, was 27. Their love story began with mutual attraction but soon blossomed into a professional partnership that would redefine both their lives. Together, they formed the duo Sonny & Cher, and their success was meteoric. Their marriage, however, was far from perfect. While their professional lives soared, their personal relationship struggled. The pressures of fame and the dynamics of their public persona began to strain their bond, leading to their separation in 1974, just over a decade after their whirlwind marriage.

Sonny and Cher's divorce was highly publicized, and Cher's emotional journey through the end of her marriage was something many could relate to. The dissolution of their relationship was painful, but Cher, ever resilient, used it as an opportunity to rediscover herself. She had two children with Sonny, Chastity (now Chaz) and a son named Elijah Blue, both of whom she raised with great devotion. Despite their divorce, Cher and Sonny's relationship remained somewhat amicable. She once remarked that despite everything, Sonny remained the person she loved the most at the time.

After her divorce from Sonny, Cher didn't let heartbreak keep her from seeking out love again. In 1975, she married Gregg Allman, the frontman of the Allman Brothers Band, in a short-lived but intense union. Their relationship was marked by both passion and turmoil. Much like her marriage to Sonny, Cher's time with Gregg was fraught with challenges. Allman's struggles with addiction and his rocky lifestyle contributed to the unraveling of their marriage. Cher gave birth to their son, Elijah Blue, but the marriage ended in 1977, after just three years. The relationship was full of highs and lows, but Cher's ability to move forward and raise her children amid the difficulties showed her strength as a mother and individual. She later reflected that her time with Gregg, though challenging, was a learning experience that helped her grow in new ways.

Despite two high-profile marriages, Cher's romantic life continued to be a topic of fascination throughout the years. She's had several relationships in the decades that followed, though she never remarried. She found love with several famous figures, but none of these relationships reached the depth or longevity of her first two marriages. One of her most publicized relationships was with Tom Cruise in the 1980s, a brief but memorable pairing that turned heads. The two were spotted together frequently during their time as a couple, though the relationship was short-lived. Cher later admitted that despite their passionate connection, their differing careers and lifestyles made it difficult for the relationship to last. It was just another chapter in her love life that was over almost as quickly as it had begun, but it left a lasting impression on the public.

Over the years, Cher has also had relationships with other famous figures, including the actor Val Kilmer and billionaire philanthropist Craig W. Smith. Her ability to keep much of her personal life private despite being one of the world's most famous women speaks to her desire for independence and privacy. While many public figures would be eager to keep their relationships under constant scrutiny, Cher took a different approach. She shared just enough to satisfy public curiosity but maintained control over what she revealed.

Her relationships with her children have always been the central focus of her personal life. Cher has often said that her children, especially Chaz, are her greatest accomplishments. She has supported Chaz through significant challenges, including Chaz's gender transition. Cher's openness and support for Chaz, who became the first openly transgender man to appear on the cover of *People* magazine, is a powerful example of her commitment to unconditional love. She stood by Chaz during his transition, not just as a mother but as a fierce advocate for LGBTQ+ rights. This relationship has been one of the most important and meaningful of Cher's life, and she has spoken often about how it shaped her views on love, identity, and family. Through her support of Chaz, Cher has shown the world what true love and acceptance look like, and in doing so, has become a role model for others who may be navigating their own complex family dynamics.

Cher's relationships, both romantic and familial, reflect the complexities of a woman who, despite her fame, has faced many of the same challenges as others. She has experienced the joy and pain that come with falling in and out of love, the challenges of raising children while juggling a high-profile career, and the difficulties of navigating public expectations. Despite the ups and downs, she has always remained true to herself. While she never found lasting romantic love after her marriages to Sonny and Gregg, her strength and resilience have inspired countless fans who admire her for being unapologetically herself, no matter what life throws her way.

Cher's relationships serve as a reminder that love isn't always straightforward, and sometimes it's the challenges that help us grow. Whether through marriage, family, or her relationships with friends and partners, Cher has demonstrated that love, in all its forms, is worth pursuing, even if it doesn't always go as planned. Her story is one of resilience, growth, and unwavering love for her family.

Raising Children in the Spotlight

Cher's journey as a mother, raising her children in the glare of the public spotlight, has been one filled with both challenges and triumphs. She became a mother at a young age, giving birth to her first child, Chastity (now Chaz), with Sonny Bono in 1969. As a young mother, Cher was thrust into the world of fame and media attention almost immediately. Despite the overwhelming pressure of being constantly in the public eye, she did her best to give her children the kind of love and stability they needed, all while maintaining her career and staying true to herself.

From the very beginning, Cher was committed to being a hands-on mother. Though her professional life took her across the world, she always made time for her children. As a single mother after her divorce from Sonny, Cher faced the added challenge of raising her children without the support of a partner. But despite the emotional strain that came with the breakdown of her marriage, Cher remained a constant presence in her children's lives. In interviews, she has often reflected on how important it was for her to maintain a close relationship with Chaz and Elijah Blue, and how she did everything she could to ensure they grew up with a sense of security and love.

Raising children while navigating a high-profile career meant that Cher had to strike a delicate balance. The constant media attention often focused not just on her work but also on her family life. The pressure to be both an artist and a mother was immense, but Cher found a way to make it work. She spoke openly about the challenges of balancing motherhood with her responsibilities as an entertainer, often stating that while it was difficult, it was also incredibly rewarding. She believed in being involved in every aspect of her children's lives, from their education to their emotional well-being, while also making sure they were never shielded from the realities of her own fame.

As Chaz grew older, Cher supported him through what would become one of the most significant transitions in his life—the decision to live as a man. Chaz's gender transition was a deeply personal journey, and Cher's role as a mother during this time was crucial. She stood by Chaz unconditionally, providing a strong and loving support system as he navigated the challenges of transitioning publicly. In many ways, Cher's relationship with Chaz is a testament to her ability to accept her children for who they are, no matter what.

Cher has spoken extensively about how proud she is of Chaz and his courage in living authentically. While the media sometimes sensationalized Chaz's transition, Cher remained steadfast in her support, going out of her way to speak positively about her child's decision to live as his true self. Her advocacy for Chaz during this time extended beyond just their family. Cher has been vocal about the importance of LGBTQ+ rights and inclusion, using her platform to raise awareness and promote acceptance for the transgender community. She has often said that her role as a mother made her a stronger advocate for Chaz's rights, understanding firsthand the importance of unconditional love and support.

Raising Elijah Blue, her second child with ex-husband Gregg Allman, presented its own set of challenges. Elijah, like Chaz, grew up in the shadow of his famous mother, but he has largely stayed out of the limelight, preferring to live a more private life. Cher has always respected Elijah's need for privacy, and the two share a close relationship, with Cher expressing pride in Elijah's artistic talents and his own success as a musician. While Elijah has pursued a career in music, he has done so on his own terms, stepping out of Cher's massive shadow. Cher's support of Elijah's pursuits, much like with Chaz, has been unwavering.

Despite the media's fascination with her family, Cher has always been protective of her children's privacy. She has spoken about how difficult it is to shield them from the public's constant scrutiny, especially when it comes to their personal lives. Yet, she also acknowledges that her fame meant they could never truly be anonymous, and that made her efforts to shield them from negativity all the more important. Cher has often used her platform to speak about the difficulties of raising children in the public eye, acknowledging how it was hard for her kids to deal with the inevitable judgment that came with being her child.

But Cher also knew how important it was to maintain her role as a mother while also encouraging her children to pursue their passions. She has always been incredibly proud of Chaz's and Elijah Blue's independent achievements, from Chaz's advocacy work to Elijah's career in music. Throughout all of her personal and professional achievements, Cher never lost sight of her primary role as a mother. She has often said that being a mom was her greatest job, and no amount of fame or fortune could ever change that.

The public's interest in Cher's children has not been without its difficulties, but it's clear that Cher has always been steadfast in her devotion to them. She has successfully raised two children who have both found their own paths in life, despite the immense pressure that came with being raised by one of the most famous women in the world. Cher's willingness to be open and vulnerable about her experiences as a mother has given her fans a glimpse into the human side of her celebrity life.

Her relationship with her children serves as a powerful reminder that, no matter how successful or famous one may become, family remains at the core of everything. Cher has always made sure to keep her children close, allowing them the space they need to grow into their own individuals while providing them with a stable, loving foundation. Through her dedication, resilience, and unconditional love, Cher has proven time and again that, for her, being a mother has been the most rewarding experience of all.

The Bond with Her Late Mother, Georgia Holt

Cher's relationship with her mother, Georgia Holt, was one that transcended the typical mother-daughter bond, filled with both deep love and challenges, and shaped much of Cher's own understanding of motherhood. Georgia, a woman who was often described as strong, independent, and with her own dreams of stardom, played a significant role in shaping Cher's character, values, and aspirations.

Georgia Holt, born in 1926 in the small town of Kensett, Arkansas, was a woman ahead of her time. She was a talented singer and actress, and though she did not find the same level of fame as her daughter, her own career in entertainment proved to be a crucial influence on Cher's early life. Cher, who grew up in a turbulent household with multiple relocations, watched her mother chase her own dreams of stardom. In fact, Georgia's resilience in the face of numerous obstacles—whether it was the breakdown of marriages or the struggles she faced as an aspiring artist—left an indelible impression on Cher.

From a very young age, Cher was exposed to the world of entertainment, which her mother navigated with tenacity. Despite Georgia's personal struggles, she was committed to providing for her children, especially Cher, who was often the focus of Georgia's dreams. Cher recalled that her mother was very open with her about the hardships of being a woman in the entertainment industry, and it was through those conversations that Cher learned the value of determination, self-reliance, and resilience.

Georgia Holt was a complex figure in Cher's life. As a mother, she was sometimes demanding and at other times distant, but Cher always held deep admiration for her. In interviews, Cher has described her relationship with her mother as both challenging and beautiful. Cher often said that her mother's tough love approach was essential in shaping her into the woman she became. Georgia had high expectations for Cher, and though their relationship wasn't always smooth, Cher credited her mother for teaching her how to stand up for herself and for showing her what it meant to be an independent woman.

One of the most significant aspects of Cher's bond with Georgia was their shared experience of hardship. Georgia's own journey to stardom was a complicated one, marked by a series of struggles, including financial instability and unfulfilled dreams of becoming a major recording artist. But rather than be defeated by these setbacks, Georgia Holt pushed forward, taking on whatever work was available, whether it was singing in nightclubs, acting in small roles, or later, working as a voice coach. Through it all, Georgia taught Cher that success doesn't always come easily and that determination in the face of adversity is one of the most important qualities to possess.

Despite her own unfulfilled dreams, Georgia always supported Cher's career, even when it meant putting her own aspirations aside. She was one of Cher's biggest supporters during the early years of her rise to fame, helping her navigate the pressures of the entertainment world while also offering practical advice. Cher often spoke about the strong bond she had with her mother, noting that their relationship was built on mutual respect. Cher, who often had to be her own cheerleader in the entertainment business, found comfort in knowing that her mother was always rooting for her. Their shared experiences as women trying to break through in a male-dominated industry created a bond that was uniquely strong.

As Cher's career grew, she continued to stay close to Georgia, even though her fame made it difficult for them to lead normal lives. Cher was extremely protective of her mother and made sure that she had the care and attention she needed, especially as Georgia faced health issues in her later years. Cher even took on the role of primary caregiver when Georgia began to suffer from various health problems, including a battle with cancer. Cher's dedication to her mother in her final years was a testament to the deep love and respect she had for her.

Beyond being a caregiver, Cher also made it a priority to ensure that Georgia had opportunities to showcase her own talent. In 2013, at the age of 87, Georgia Holt finally released her own album, "Honky Tonk Woman," which Cher helped produce. It was a moment of validation for Georgia, who had spent most of her life supporting her daughter's dreams while quietly shelving her own. For Cher, it was a way to honor her mother's legacy and to allow her mother the chance to have her moment in the spotlight.

The bond between Cher and her late mother has remained a deeply emotional aspect of Cher's life. After Georgia's passing in 2022, Cher shared on social media how much she missed her mother and how her death had left a profound impact on her. Cher's emotional tributes to her mother reflected not only a daughter's love for her mother but also the complex and multifaceted relationship that had been built over a lifetime. Cher had always spoken about how much she admired her mother's strength, and in her later years, she came to appreciate her more deeply than ever before. The love they shared was profound, and Cher often expressed how she felt like a part of her was gone after her mother's death.

The passing of Georgia Holt was also a reminder of the legacy she left behind. Cher has frequently credited her mother with being a source of inspiration and strength throughout her life and career. Georgia's ability to face hardship with dignity and to keep fighting for what she wanted, despite many obstacles, has stayed with Cher, even after her mother's passing. In many ways, Georgia Holt was the model for the kind of resilience and grace that Cher embodies in her own life. Their bond, filled with love, challenges, and triumphs, was a testament to the powerful relationship between a mother and daughter, and it will continue to influence Cher's life long after Georgia's death.

10

Cher Today

Life Beyond the Spotlight

True love is not about finding someone to live with, it's about finding someone you can't imagine living without." Cher has long lived by this philosophy, and her journey through the decades has reflected this belief, whether in her relationships, her career, or her approach to life beyond the stage. Today, Cher is not only a legendary figure in the entertainment industry but also an individual who continues to inspire millions with her resilience, charisma, and refusal to age in a world that often defines people by their years.

In recent years, Cher has embraced her personal life in ways that reflect both a love for adventure and a desire for peace. She has often spoken about her ability to enjoy solitude, finding joy in simple pleasures that most people may overlook. Cher has spent much of her time traveling, visiting places that spark her interest and pushing herself to explore new experiences, whether that's through charity work, discovering new passions, or spending time with family and close friends. This shift toward more personal fulfillment marks a significant departure from the constant hustle of the entertainment industry that once defined her. But Cher's impact on the world remains as strong as ever.

One of the defining characteristics of Cher's post-career life is her commitment to philanthropy. For years, she has used her platform to raise awareness for numerous causes, including supporting charities that focus on human rights, animal welfare, and health-related issues. She has long been an advocate for the LGBTQ+ community, leveraging her iconic status to promote equality and justice for those who often feel marginalized. Whether through social media, her public statements, or her participation in charity events, Cher continues to be a voice for the voiceless, a champion of the underdog.

Beyond her public efforts to make a difference, Cher has also found comfort in focusing on her own well-being, shifting away from the pressures of the entertainment industry. As someone who has faced so much scrutiny over the years—whether it was for her physical appearance, her career choices, or her relationships—Cher now lives with a sense of peace that only comes with years of hard-earned wisdom. In fact, as she has gotten older, she has become more outspoken about embracing aging. She openly acknowledges the challenges that come with getting older, but she does so with the same sense of defiance that has marked her entire career. Cher's refusal to conform to the typical expectations of beauty and age in Hollywood has made her a role model for people of all ages who struggle with similar issues.

In her personal life, Cher has become known for her close relationships with her children, particularly her son, Chaz Bono. As a mother, Cher has always been fiercely protective and supportive, and her bond with Chaz is a testament to her growth as a person. Chaz's journey, including his public transition, has only strengthened their connection, and Cher has remained a pillar of strength for him throughout the years. In interviews, she often speaks about her deep admiration for her children and the pride she feels in their independence. Despite the pressures that come with living in the public eye, Cher has maintained a sense of normalcy within her family unit.

Cher's ability to adapt to the changing world around her is one of the reasons she continues to stay relevant. She has managed to remain part of popular culture, even as she ages, by embracing technology and engaging with her fans through social media. Despite her long history of success, Cher shows no sign of slowing down. Whether it's through her music, advocacy, or simply by sharing a glimpse into her life, she remains one of the most recognizable and influential figures in pop culture.

She has continued to release new music, often experimenting with modern sounds while staying true to her own iconic style. Cher's "Here We Go Again" tour, which celebrated her 2018 album of the same name, is just one example of how she continues to connect with audiences. The show was a massive success, both commercially and critically, and it proved that Cher's voice and stage presence still have the power to captivate fans around the world. Even in her 70s, she can still command a stage, putting on a high-energy performance that belies her age. Her ability to reinvent herself while staying true to her roots is something that has become synonymous with her career, and it's what continues to keep fans excited.

Perhaps one of the most inspiring aspects of Cher's life beyond the spotlight is her personal mantra to never settle. Whether she's been conquering new genres of music, exploring different areas of the entertainment world, or advocating for those in need, Cher's unwillingness to conform has been a guiding principle throughout her life. She's not just a pop star or a cultural icon; she's a force of nature, and she continues to push boundaries and challenge societal norms with every step she takes.

The journey from the dazzling world of music and television to the quieter, more personal side of life hasn't been an easy one, but Cher's resilience has always been what has carried her through. Even when faced with loss, challenges, and heartache, she has never given up on herself or on the people she loves. And that's part of what makes her so remarkable—she continues to inspire those around her by showing them that life is what you make of it, regardless of where you're starting from or how old you are.

As Cher continues to live life on her terms, it's clear that her journey is far from over. She remains as powerful and influential as ever, showing the world that aging is not a limitation but an opportunity to grow and redefine who you are. Cher is a testament to the power of perseverance, adaptability, and the relentless pursuit of joy. Through her music, her advocacy, and her personal growth, she continues to leave a lasting impact on the world. Her story isn't just about fame—it's about living a life filled with purpose, compassion, and the unwavering belief that it's never too late to start something new. And in this new chapter of her life, Cher continues to show us all what it means to live authentically and with unapologetic joy.

New Projects and Ventures

Cher has always been a force of nature, and even as the world changes, she continues to keep up with the times by embarking on new projects and ventures that push her boundaries and redefine what it means to be a modern-day icon. Her ability to stay relevant in an ever-changing entertainment landscape speaks to her creativity, drive, and determination. With each new endeavor, Cher proves that she's not only a star of the past, but a shining example of how to build a future that remains impactful and fresh, regardless of the years.

In recent years, Cher has dabbled in a variety of ventures that go beyond music and film. She's continued to build her brand and reach new audiences by expanding her influence into other industries. One notable area of focus has been her involvement in the business world, where she has capitalized on her star power and iconic status. Cher has partnered with various brands, lending her name and her creative touch to everything from fashion lines to fragrance collections. In one of her most high-profile ventures, Cher launched a line of wigs and beauty products designed for women who want to embrace their individuality, offering a glimpse into her ever-evolving relationship with beauty and style. These projects not only give her a chance to express herself in new ways but also connect her with fans who admire her style and unique approach to self-expression.

One of Cher's more recent ventures has been her ongoing involvement in activism and social justice. She has long been an advocate for LGBTQ+ rights, but in recent years, she has taken her advocacy to new heights, supporting various causes and organizations dedicated to improving the lives of marginalized communities. Through social media and public appearances, Cher has been vocal about her desire to create change and raise awareness about important issues. Whether it's through fundraising, charity events, or simply using her platform to amplify the voices of those who need it most, Cher continues to make a difference in ways that are true to her values.

Cher's philanthropic efforts have led her to focus on humanitarian work, particularly regarding the well-being of children and families. She has worked with a number of charities aimed at providing support for vulnerable communities, ensuring that those in need have access to the resources and opportunities that can improve their lives. Whether it's through financial donations, raising awareness, or getting involved with grassroots organizations, Cher's impact has been far-reaching, and her commitment to social causes remains as strong as ever.

Despite her legendary career and long list of accomplishments, Cher has never been content to rest on her laurels. She has consistently pursued new avenues for artistic expression, including exploring new genres and styles of music. Cher has always been known for her ability to reinvent herself, and her ongoing projects show that she's still capable of surprising the world. Her latest music, which blends pop, dance, and electronic elements, represents her ability to adapt to changing trends while still staying true to the essence of who she is as an artist. Whether it's through new singles, live performances, or collaborations with other artists, Cher continues to prove that her voice is as relevant today as it ever was.

In addition to her musical career, Cher has made waves in the film industry once again, collaborating with directors and writers to take on new roles that continue to challenge her as an actress. While she's often remembered for her unforgettable performances in "Moonstruck" and "Silkwood," Cher hasn't slowed down when it comes to pursuing acting opportunities that speak to her artistic interests. As of late, she has been cast in a variety of exciting projects that span across genres, demonstrating that her versatility and experience in the industry still hold weight.

One of the most exciting projects she's embarked on recently has been her return to Broadway, where she has been involved in stage productions that showcase her musical talents in new ways. Cher's involvement in Broadway shows allows her to reconnect with her roots in live performance, all while appealing to a new audience who may not have experienced her impact through her music and television appearances. These ventures on stage not only allow her to showcase her incredible talents but also highlight her commitment to pushing herself as an artist and performer, even after decades in the industry.

Additionally, Cher's involvement with film and television is expanding into other roles behind the camera. As a producer, Cher has taken an active role in developing projects that align with her values and interests. She's been working on multiple projects in various stages of development, including films that touch on social issues and themes of empowerment. Cher has often used her platform to give voice to those who feel unheard, and through these new ventures, she's able to take that passion a step further by using her influence to shape narratives and bring important stories to life.

As she moves forward, Cher's entrepreneurial spirit continues to guide her as she diversifies her portfolio. Whether it's exploring new technologies, collaborating with fellow musicians and artists, or creating innovative projects in the entertainment world, Cher remains a trailblazer. With her timeless ability to captivate audiences, it's clear that Cher's ventures are far from over. From acting and music to activism and beyond, her endless reinvention continues to influence the entertainment industry and set a standard for other artists to follow. Cher is a true example of how someone can remain relevant and continue to make an impact even after decades in the spotlight.

Cher's Legacy

Cher's legacy is as multifaceted as her career itself, a testament to her unyielding determination, extraordinary talent, and ability to reinvent herself time and time again. From her early days as a backup singer to her current status as a global icon, Cher has shaped the entertainment landscape in ways that few others have. Her influence spans across music, film, fashion, and social activism, and her impact can still be seen in the artists and movements she inspired throughout the years.

When you think of Cher, you think of an artist who defied convention. From her deep, husky voice to her ability to shift effortlessly between genres, Cher has always been one to push boundaries. Her voice became her signature, a sound that was unlike anything heard before. She carved out a space for herself in a crowded music scene in the '60s and '70s, initially as part of the iconic duo Sonny & Cher, and later as a solo artist whose presence could not be ignored. With chart-topping hits like "I Got You Babe," "Gypsies, Tramps and Thieves," and "Believe," Cher redefined what it meant to be a pop star, using her voice and charisma to build a legacy that has endured for decades.

Cher's musical journey was groundbreaking not only because of her distinct sound but also because of her ability to evolve and stay relevant in a fast-paced industry. When music trends shifted, she adapted, constantly reinventing herself and her image to stay at the forefront. In the '80s and '90s, she transitioned from pop superstar to dance music queen, ushering in a new era with hits like "If I Could Turn Back Time" and "Believe." Her ability to continually reinvent her sound and style kept her on top of the charts and in the public eye, making her one of the few artists who managed to not just survive but thrive in an ever-changing musical landscape.

Beyond music, Cher's legacy is inextricably linked to her work in Hollywood. Few artists have made the transition from pop icon to respected actress with such ease and success. Her performances in "Silkwood," "Moonstruck," and "Mask" showcased a depth and versatility that surprised many who initially only knew her as a singer. Her Oscar win for "Moonstruck" solidified her place in the pantheon of great actresses and proved that she was more than just a pop star. But it wasn't just her acting that made an impact—it was her ability to craft characters that resonated with audiences, characters who were often complex, strong-willed, and unapologetically themselves, much like Cher herself.

What makes Cher truly legendary is her ability to transcend the roles she's played, the music she's made, and the fashion she's worn to become a symbol of empowerment. Cher has never been one to conform to traditional standards of beauty or societal expectations. She has always celebrated individuality, whether through her bold fashion choices or her unfiltered opinions. Her style, often described as glamorous and avant-garde, has become a hallmark of her public persona, inspiring countless fans and fashion icons. From the feathered wigs and sequined gowns to her more recent edgy, chic looks, Cher has always embodied the spirit of someone who was willing to take risks and push the envelope.

Cher's influence isn't confined to her artistic achievements. She has long been a voice for marginalized communities, particularly the LGBTQ+ community, advocating for equality and rights long before it was mainstream. Her support for LGBTQ+ rights has made her a beloved figure within the community, where she is seen as a fierce ally and role model. Her willingness to speak out on issues like AIDS awareness, gender identity, and LGBTQ+ equality has solidified her status as a voice for change, using her platform to uplift and support those who need it most. Her advocacy has helped create spaces where people can feel seen and valued, something that has been central to her mission for decades.

Her humanitarian work extends beyond just one community, though. Cher's philanthropy is vast, and she has been involved in numerous charitable endeavors throughout her career, from raising funds for children's hospitals to supporting military families and advocating for animal rights. Through her involvement with various organizations, Cher has made a tangible difference in the lives of people across the world, demonstrating that her impact reaches far beyond her work in the entertainment industry.

But perhaps what makes Cher's legacy truly timeless is her ability to inspire others, particularly women, to break free from societal expectations and be unapologetically themselves. Throughout her career, Cher has defied labels, whether as a woman in a male-dominated industry or as an artist who refuses to be boxed into one genre. Her resilience in the face of personal and professional challenges has made her an icon of strength, independence, and longevity. For many, Cher represents the ultimate expression of self-determination—someone who has built a career on their own terms and has shown others how to do the same.

Cher's ability to adapt and evolve has allowed her to maintain her relevance in an industry that often discards its legends, and her willingness to be true to herself has made her an icon whose legacy will endure for generations. She has shaped the music, film, and fashion industries in ways that continue to inspire new talent and influence current trends. But more than that, Cher's legacy is one of empowerment—of encouraging others to be bold, to take risks, and to never let anyone dictate their worth. Her legacy is a testament to the power of reinvention, the importance of staying true to one's values, and the impact one individual can have on the world.

Cher is not just a legend; she is a living, breathing symbol of what it means to break the mold and defy expectations. Her legacy, built over decades of groundbreaking work and advocacy, will continue to inspire and shape the world for years to come.

Conclusion

Cher's extraordinary journey is nothing short of remarkable—a testament to resilience, reinvention, and unwavering authenticity. From her early days as a backup singer to her rise as a solo artist, film star, and global icon, she has continuously broken barriers and redefined what it means to be a performer. Through it all, she has remained true to herself, never compromising her individuality or voice, and her ability to reinvent herself with each new decade is a model of artistic and personal growth. Cher's career has not only been a series of successes, but also a journey of challenges, triumphs, and the kind of fearless determination that has made her a trailblazer in the entertainment world.

Her story teaches us that success is not a straight path but one marked by perseverance, self-belief, and a willingness to embrace change. In a world that often tries to place people in boxes, Cher has shown us the power of defying expectations. Whether it was taking on new musical styles, exploring different genres in film, or speaking out on important social issues, she has consistently used her platform to challenge conventions and inspire others to do the same. Her career has been a testament to the power of reinvention—showing us that it is possible to evolve, to take risks, and to find new ways to shine, no matter how many years have passed or how many times the world has changed.

Cher's impact goes far beyond her work as an artist. She has used her fame to advocate for important causes, standing up for marginalized communities and fighting for equality. Her advocacy for LGBTQ+ rights and her philanthropy have made her a beloved figure who is respected not just for her artistic achievements but also for her compassion and commitment to making the world a better place. Her courage to speak out for what she believes in, even when it wasn't popular, has made her a symbol of strength and integrity.

Cher has also taught us the importance of embracing our unique selves. Her journey is one of self-expression—of refusing to conform to societal norms and instead celebrating the power of individuality. She has shown us that it's okay to take up space, to be bold, and to chase after what you truly want, regardless of the obstacles that may arise. She is an enduring symbol of the fact that you don't have to fit into anyone else's idea of success or beauty; you just have to be yourself, unapologetically and with confidence.

As we look back on Cher's career, it's clear that her legacy will endure for generations to come. Not just through her music, films, and fashion, but through the lives she has touched and the inspiration she has provided to countless individuals around the world. Her story is one of resilience, reminding us that no matter the hardships we face, we have the power to overcome them and reinvent ourselves along the way. It is also a story of empowerment, showing us that we are capable of achieving great things when we remain true to who we are. Cher's extraordinary journey is an enduring lesson in the power of reinvention, resilience, and living authentically—a legacy that will continue to inspire, uplift, and teach future generations for years to come.

Dear Reader,

Thank you for taking the time to explore this book. Your journey through Cher's incredible life and career is a reflection of her unique story, and I hope it has inspired and resonated with you as much as it did with me while writing it. Cher has been an icon for decades, and her story is one of resilience, reinvention, and the power of staying true to oneself. It's been an honor to share this journey with you.

If you've enjoyed reading, I'd be truly grateful if you could take a moment to leave a review or rating on Amazon. Your feedback not only helps me, but it also guides other readers in discovering the magic of this story. Whether it's a quick rating or a thoughtful review, every bit of your input goes a long way in helping this book reach others who can appreciate it just as you have.

Thank you once again for your support. It means the world to me, and I can't wait to hear your thoughts on Cher's remarkable journey!

With gratitude,
CLAIRE MORSE

Printed in Great Britain
by Amazon